ANGER MANAGEMENT

A Practical Guide

ADRIAN FAUPEL

ELIZABETH HERRICK

and PETER SHARP

David Fulton Publishers

London

David Fulton Publishers Ltd
414 Chiswick High Road, London W4 5TF

www.fultonpublishers.co.uk

First published in Great Britain by David Fulton Publishers 1998
10 9

British Library Cataloguing in Publication Data
A catalogue record for this book is available from the British Library.

ISBN 1–85346–562–3

Typeset by FSH Print and Production Ltd, London
Printed and bound in Great Britain by Ashford Colour Press

Contents

Acknowledgements

The authors would like to thank their colleague psychologists in Southampton and Hampshire for their ideas and support; the ideas have been incorporated into our thinking, and frequently directly into the text.

Many of the materials have been trialled in schools and the authors have run numerous anger management groups for children referred with 'problem anger'. Our thanks go to the headteachers, staff and pupils of those schools for their enthusiastic participation in these groups, which inspired us to write the book.

We would also like to thank senior officers in Southampton and Hampshire Local Education Authorities for supporting this project and recognising the need to promote emotional literacy at the same time as 'conventional' literacy and numeracy.

Many thanks to Janita Hendricks for all her hard work on the manuscript and for her good-natured tolerance as we asked for the umpteenth revision!

Personal thanks go to our partners and families; warm thanks from Adrian to Diane Solecki, from Liz Herrick to Rick Brown, and from Peter Sharp to Lindsey, Chloe and Poppy Sharp. Your support and encouragement has been a great help – and we all continue to try and manage our own anger more effectively.

Adrian Faupel
Liz Herrick
Peter Sharp
March 1998

WHAT IS ANGER?

Chapter 1

Introduction

I get angry when I want to,
I get angry when I don't,
I'll get angry when I'll try to,
I'll get angry when I won't.

I get angry when I'm threatened,
I get angry when I'm sad,
but I get angry when I'm happy,
and that just makes me mad!

Anger is a good thing,
and then again it's bad,
so now we've got it sorted,
I'm really feeling glad.

Anger engenders mixed emotions. It often leaves us feeling wrecked, or racked with guilt. There is a view that to be emotionally literate means expressing a whole range of feelings, but anger is potentially our most dangerous emotion and at its most extreme can lead to death. Contrast this with Freud's view that unexpressed anger actually causes depression, and it becomes clear that the contradictions in the poem above are very real for us all. So what is anger?

When anger is defined as 'extreme displeasure' (*Concise Oxford Dictionary*), it fails to convey the full force of the effects of anger both on the person *being angry* and on anyone on the *receiving end of the anger* or merely witnessing it as a passive observer. To compound the confusion, anger is taken to be an *emotion* and hence is further defined by the Oxford Dictionary as an 'instinctive feeling as opposed to reason'. Add to this a widely held view that anger is a negative emotion and it is perhaps easy to see why children may be bewildered by adult reaction to their anger, which is usually to extinguish it or to punish them for having the feeling in the first place.

In this book we're choosing to view anger as a *secondary emotion* that may arise from a primary emotion such as fear. Fear may in turn be bound up with embarrassment, disappointment, injury, exploitation, envy, or loss. All of these feelings represent a *threat* of some kind, albeit that we often don't recognise this while angry. If anger becomes significantly disruptive in a child's life, this may lead to emotional illiteracy. This is likely to persist through adulthood unless support is offered and accepted. This emotional illiteracy will frequently manifest itself in adult life as a failure to form or sustain meaningful relationships, and at worst may lead to a vicious circle involving violence to self or others.

Secondly, anger will be considered as a *reflection of emotional difficulties* which may lead to, or arise from, emotional disorder. For children, the roots of such disorder are often known to teachers, parents, carers and others, but less frequently, do they receive a planned and sophisticated response. Institutionally we have become increasingly adept at identifying, assessing and responding to learning difficulties but are far less adept at doing the same for emotional or behavioural difficulties.

Thirdly, anger will be considered as an *instrumental behaviour* which achieves particular outcomes and may be part of what some writers describe as conduct disorder. It can be seen as attention-seeking behaviour, or perhaps better described as attention-needing behaviour since the anger is expressed usually as a result of lack of positive attention in a child's formative years.

So, anger will be considered as an essential part of being human, and accepted as having an evolutionary or adaptive significance and a recognition, too, that anger can be either useful and positive, or harmful and negative. Aristotle's challenge, as described in Daniel Goleman's brilliant book *Emotional Intelligence*, perfectly describes this perplexing and fundamental dichotomy:

> Anyone can become angry – that is easy. But to be angry with the right person, to the right degree, at the right time, for the right purpose, and in the right way – this is not easy.
> (Aristotle, The Nicomachean Ethics, Goleman 1995)

Aristotle's challenge is to manage our emotional life with intelligence, and Goleman eloquently argues that 'we have gone too far in emphasising the value and import of the purely rational – what IQ measures – in human life. Intelligence can come to nothing when emotions hold sway.' Whilst one angry child resembles another at the level of physiological response, the way in which each adapts, to and controls their feelings of rage differs widely according to upbringing and personal traits. Currently little work is done with parents to make them more effective, and, arguably, even less with teachers to help them in their work with children. This book seeks to offer advice and guidance to teachers, parents, and other emotionally intelligent readers on how to manage anger – our own, and the anger of other adults and children.

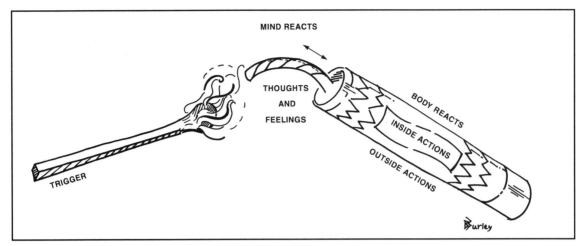

Figure 1.1 The Firework Model. Adapted from Novaco's model for Anger Arousal by Fiendler and Ecton 1986

The *trigger* is the match that ignites a person's fuse	The *fuse* is the mind reacting – thoughts/feelings (e.g. fear/threat)	The *explosive cylinder* is the body responding physiologically and may lead to anger being expressed.

Figure 1.1 is a useful model for understanding how anger occurs; it is adapted from Novaco's Model for Anger Arousal (Feindler and Ecton 1986). The Firework Model has proven particularly accessible and memorable to young children, adolescents, and indeed the adults that we have worked with in running anger management groups in recent years.

When presented with a three-dimensional representation of the Firework Model, even young infants seem able to grasp the notion of avoiding triggers (such as people, situations, times, words) or else minimising or reducing their impact, by being able to rethink or reframe their reaction to triggers, and either lengthen their fuse or extinguish it before explosion! Later in the book we will return to show how this model may be used to support anger management groupwork with children and young people.

If the Firework Model is a schematic representation at the individual level, showing what happens to me when I get angry, then the metaphor of a 'storm' may help to describe anger in terms of the 'bigger picture', where environmental influences are as important as the reaction of the individual. Storms occur, and will go on occurring, but there are ways to avoid storms or to minimise their impact, and certainly to weather them and deal with any aftermath.

Some storms are heralded by well-understood indicators, such as gathering clouds and changes in pressure or wind direction, light

Figure 1.2 *'The storm'*

fading or sudden darkness. So it is with some angry outbursts or violent incidents, for example when teachers report that they know what kind of a day a class or pupil are going to have simply from the way they enter a room first thing in the morning. Clearly then, avoidance strategies will be of great help in trying to head-off a storm, or go round it rather than through it. We will look more closely at planning to avoid a storm in Chapter 5.

Some storms appear to be 'unannounced' and both teachers and parents will sometimes describe children's anger as appearing 'out of the blue'. Here the emphasis must be on weathering the storm, and strategies for parents and teachers might include defusing the anger at the point of difficulty and before the anger becomes dangerous. We will consider how to do this in Chapter 6.

Storms are inevitable, even where strategies have been tried to either avoid or weather them. So strategies for clearing up after the storm, learning from the experience and planning to reduce the likelihood of a similar storm will be explored in Chapter 7.

In Chapter 8 we address the important issue of working with very angry children, including tactical advice and guidance, and will go on in Chapter 9 to acknowledge that we can not get it right all the time, especially if the anger is made less predictable by drugs, alcohol or psychosis.

Specific advice for parents is offered in Chapter 10, though we hope parents will be encouraged to read the rest of the book by what you find there!

For readers intending to use the book as a resource for running groups, or for teaching, the Appendices 1 to 9 include numerous freely photocopiable sheets.

Chapter 2

Perspectives on anger

To understand and to manage anger is no easy task as it involves a complex interaction of thoughts, feelings and behaviour. It is the action and behaviour which cause damage to oneself and to others, so it becomes essential to understand what causes or influences that behaviour.

The Firework Model is a simple and effective way to understand what happens when people get angry, but a deeper understanding of the related issues will be obtained by considering a range of perspectives.

Psychologists have differed in the ways they have seen the three components, thinking, feeling and behaviour, interacting, and this has influenced the way they have seen how such behaviour should be managed or controlled. The following accounts are necessarily somewhat oversimplified, but they at least reflect the relative emphasis that psychologists have given to each of the three components.

The Behaviourist approach sees 'Behaviour' as primary (Figure 2.1), in that it is the way we behave that really matters. Behaviourists believe that behaviour is controlled by the past history of rewards and punishments given to particular behaviour – as a general rule, there is a greater probability of my hitting somebody if that hitting is reinforced by somebody immediately complying with my demand and giving me their sweets. Behaviour which is followed by an aversive consequence is less likely to be repeated.

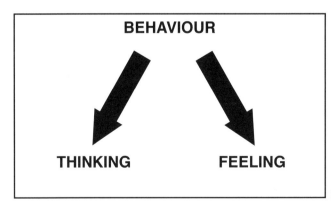

Figure 2.1 Behaviourist approach

7

Another way of viewing the likelihood of behaviour occurring is described by the 'ABC Model' which is frequently used as a behaviour management tool in schools. Technically this is known as the Functional Analysis of Behaviour for it sees Behaviour (B) as a function of the Antecedents (A) and the Consequences (C). This means that if either the antecedents of the behaviour, or its consequences (or both), are changed, the probability of that behaviour happening will also be changed. The antecedents are particularly important in preventative aspects of controlling difficult behaviour. The triggers provoking anger can be such things as irritants (noise, overcrowding, heat) and these are clearly environmental aspects which can often be changed. Other antecedents are to do with the way demands are made of people; the way a teacher tells a pupil off for example can 'provoke' an angry reaction. Another teacher, with a different style achieves the same effect but without cornering the pupil. The way demands are made to pupils can also provoke a different reaction. Whole school policies also fit into this antecedent framework – schools which have very clearly articulated boundaries of what is acceptable behaviour and what is not, consistently seem to experience less abuse and aggressive behaviour.

Rewards and punishments are clearly used extensively in schools and families to 'control' pupils' behaviour. In a preventative sense, school policies should articulate very clearly how pupil's appropriate prosocial behaviour will be noticed, acknowledged and rewarded and how inappropriate antisocial behaviour will be discouraged. There has been a gradual revolution in school behaviour policies as they try to focus on the former these days, at least as much as the latter.

The behaviourist approach also reminds us that social behaviours are learnt in the same way as any other behaviours. This is frequently forgotten by teachers who leap to consider rewards and consequences when a pupil is producing angry, aggressive and uncontrolled behaviour which hurts other people. When a child has a reading difficulty we do not start off by considering rewards and punishments. We appropriately ask: does the child know what to do, then does he or she know *how* to do it, and then have they had enough practice at doing it. Only if all of these questions have been answered in the affirmative, do we question the child's motivation and then try to make it more worthwhile (by the judicial use of incentives and sanctions). When it comes to social and interpersonal behaviour, we frequently forget that we should be asking the same questions in the same order – instead we simply ascribe dubious motivation and rush into rewards and punishments. The Social Skills model discussed in Chapter 8 is derived originally from a behaviourist approach.

Figure 2.2 shows a rather different arrangement of the

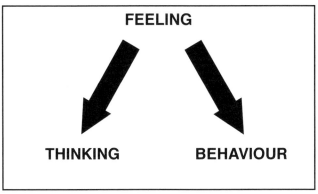

Figure 2.2 *Psychodynamic approach*

relationships between feelings, thinking and behaviour. These approaches emphasise the primacy of feelings or emotions which drive our behaviour. Amongst them are the psychodynamic approaches, first described by Sigmund Freud. Central to Freud's understanding of difficult behaviour are the 'defence mechanisms', which are designed to protect us from unacceptable, and anxiety-provoking, impulses reaching consciousness. When they threaten to do so, we experience high levels of anxiety. In order to protect ourselves against this anxiety we adopt one or more of possible strategies or 'mechanisms'. A more popular word for this anxiety is 'stress', which can be considered as threats to our self-esteem, when our personal basic needs are not being met. Such stress produces very aversive 'negative' emotions, which include anger. One of the defence mechanisms described by Freud is 'displacement' and the application of this to anger is clear to see. The anger vented by a bully on a defenceless and weak classmate may be displaced from anger which 'should' be directed to an abusing parent. But this raises so much anxiety, that the anger becomes displaced onto the victim.

Other important Freudian ideas can be very useful for the teacher, both in understanding their own angry emotions to children (and staff!) and children's anger itself. They include 'transference' and 'projection'. We carry around with us a vast amount of emotional baggage and 'unfinished business' in which are found attitudes (for example to authority, to women, or to men) laid down in our unique early emotional history. Freud's notion of transference reminds us of the irrationality of our emotional reactions to people and events.

A development of psychodynamic thinking by John Bowlby (1978) also emphasised the importance of emotions in his attachment theory. At its heart is the notion of a secure emotional base which all children need and from which they begin to explore the interpersonal world around them. This early security and bonding is crucial to the growth of mature interdependence, which begins in childhood and continues through adolescence and into adulthood. When this sense of security is threatened, very disturbing and aversive emotions are experienced, leading sometimes to desperate attempts to re-establish contact with emotional security. Anger is one of the felt responses to a threat to security – as any parent may have experienced when instead of loving embraces after a prolonged absence, he or she is met with a 'calculated' and punishing coldness! Attachment theory reminds us of the importance of 'belonging', which again links us with a feeling of being valued or loveable and so with self-esteem. The litmus paper of a school's effectiveness can be described in terms of whether the school really does convey a sense of community, belonging and value to all its pupils. If any children do not achieve this sense of security, expressions of angry, hostile and destructive behaviour are more likely.

The third component to which psychologists give relative emphasis is that of thinking or the cognitive dimension, (Figure 2.3). Cognitive psychologists believe that the nature of thinking heavily influences the emotions that we feel, and it is these emotions which then drive our behaviour. There are two ways in which thinking or thought processes can do this. The first of these considers how our thinking can become distorted or irrational, leading to negative emotions, including anger.

Psychologists adopting this approach, usually called 'cognitive behavioural psychologists', start with the belief that it is not what happens to us which makes us angry, or sad, or depressed, etc. The same dreadful event can happen to several people, yet their individual reactions to it can differ remarkably. What seems to account for this difference is the way the event is viewed, rather than the event itself. Douglas Bader, who lived for flying, lost both his legs. His reaction was to see this as a personal challenge. Another person may well have crumpled up in a state of hopeless depression, feeling bitter and twisted that life had dealt such a cruel and unfair blow. Cognitive behaviourists maintain that nothing makes us angry – in reality, it is we ourselves who make us so, by interpreting what happens to us as an attack on us, as being unjustified, unfair. The moment we *interpret* something as hostile, we become physiologically aroused. This arousal is accompanied

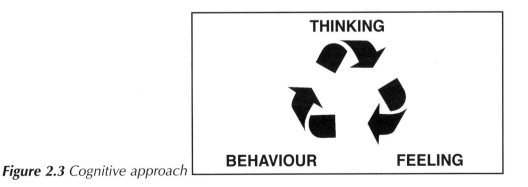

Figure 2.3 Cognitive approach

by a strong emotional urge to fight back aggressively, in other words anger.

An everyday example might help to illustrate the process. Wearing brand new leather shoes one day, one of the authors was waiting at a bus stop. Somebody stepped back and painfully stepped on those expensive new shoes, and what is more, deeply scratched the leather uppers! If he had interpreted this as being a quite deliberate act, he would undoubtedly have become very angry. How he might have expressed this anger may well have depended on whether the person was muscular and six foot six tall or not! Alternatively, he may have interpreted the misdemeanour as being due to a clumsy carelessness – he would probably then have been more irritated than angry. How he expressed that irritation, or didn't, may well have been due to the kind of moral inhibitions he had imbibed from his family upbringing. In fact, the person who stepped back was a young mother with two children, one of whom was a young toddler, and it was in controlling the toddler that caused the accident. Now, we have cause for regret rather than anger, because the damage was not seen as being hostile or due to clumsy carelessness.

One way to control anger, then, is to prevent angry feelings by changing the way we interpret the 'triggers' that normally spark these feelings off. The event is the 'match' in our Firework Model, the way we interpret the event is the 'fuse'. If we interpret the trigger as an attack, then certainly the fuse will be well and truly lit, whereas if we construe the trigger as an unfortunate accident (and do not irrationally believe that accidents should never happen to us), the fuse will be snuffed out and the explosion prevented.

What is important then is the quality of our thinking and our beliefs. It seems that people who experience negative emotions, tend to think in certain ways. Aaron Beck (1988) calls this thinking 'distorted', which is rigid, all or nothing, black and white kind of thinking. To help angry people control their anger, it is necessary to find out what they are saying to themselves, their internal dialogue when they are confronted with something that 'makes' them angry. What we find is that their thinking is of the kind described above. Albert Ellis (1994), takes a slightly different view and focuses rather on the beliefs that people hold, finding that angry people have what he calls 'irrational beliefs'. Many of the triggers which spark off anger do so because we irrationally believe that our worth and value depends upon what other people think, say and do to us. Name calling, or racial taunting, for example, has nothing to do with my real worth and value. If I really believed that, it would be very hard to become worked up because of what is said to or about me. One of aggressive children's common irrational beliefs is 'It isn't fair'. The world, has, however, never been fair and never will be. If children believe it, and adults frequently encourage them in such an erroneous view, then it is highly likely that they will become very angry when someone is perceived to have treated them unfairly – and for that he or she should be utterly condemned for daring to do so, and I'll show them how!

Cognitive behavioural psychologists focus on this distorted thinking and irrational beliefs. We know that adolescent boys who are more than usually aggressive attribute hostile intentions to what are in fact 'neutral' actions. They are hypersensitive to criticism, likely to flare up and fly off the handle. There are men serving life sentences in prison for murder because someone 'stared' at them.

There is a second way in which our thinking can affect our behaviour. Kenneth Dodge (1986), an American researcher into aggressive behaviour, sees the problem not so much to do with what we think, but in the way we think – the processes of thinking. When we enter into any social situation we immediately have tasks to achieve. It may be to face someone who has hurt us, or vice versa, or to join a group at a party, or to handle teasing. Our first task is to 'read' what is going on. We have to take in a fantastic amount of information very, very quickly whenever we enter into any social situation – people's facial expressions, tone of voice, body posture as well as myriad pieces of information about the context, not to forget information about our own feelings as well. The analysis of this information clarifies the task we have to do – the 'problem' that we have to solve. Kenneth Dodge sees us rather like computers who have to process vast amounts of information very quickly and then work out what we want to do and how to do it. Normally, all this process is out of our awareness. Rather like a chess-playing computer, we generate very quickly a series of alternative courses of action, rapidly running through their pros and cons and eventually choosing a course of action which we hope will achieve our task.

Two aspects of this process can cause us problems. First we can get into a habit of choosing one particular alternative, and thus it becomes the first we consider; secondly, some of us choose that first course of action without considering any of the others. Angry people are typically very impulsive, and there is considerable evidence that young people with emotional difficulties find it very difficult to generate alternative courses of action. They tend to get hooked on one – one that is not usually very successful.

Having chosen a particular alternative, a chess-playing computer then automatically executes a sub-routine. This is the application stage, and things can go wrong here as well. Working with a group of delinquent adolescents, we were trying to teach them alternative ways of handling teachers and police, who not infrequently had to tick them off. The boys only seemed to have one 'choice' – that of swearing back at the authority figures, which of course landed them into even deeper trouble. We were trying to get them to consider the pros and cons of alternatives, including adopting a friendly smile. When they tried this, it proved disastrous! What they thought they were doing and what they were actually doing was very different. When we videoed them practising this, it became clear that their smiles were grimaces and sneers – and hence more 'provoking' to adults then even swearing might have been.

The information-processing approach tries to establish where the problem-solving process is breaking down for the individual angry person. Is it that they cannot accurately read the situation, or that they are unable to generate alternative courses of action, or that they haven't the social skills to carry out the strategy they have chosen? These skills of problem solving and social skills can be taught directly and can become an important part of anger management training.

It is clear that each of the approaches we have outlined has something of use to offer. To focus exclusively on one thinking, feeling or behaviour component to the complete exclusion of the other two is likely to lead to less effective ways of helping children and young people learn how to manage their anger. A thorough individual assessment of the history, type and circumstances of anger is necessary to choose the most appropriate way to help.

In the next chapter we will consider what happens to us when we get angry, and explore the long-term effects of problem anger on ourselves and others.

Summary

- There are three components to anger:

  thinking

  feeling

  behaviour

- The three major perspectives in understanding anger are:

  behavioural

  psychodynamic

  cognitive–behavioural

They differ in the relative importance each one gives to the three components.

Chapter 3

What does anger do to you?

Anger is always a reaction to something, but this does not necessarily mean something *real* out there is *causing* my anger. Angry people often react angrily to what are very minor 'hurts' – but they think they have been offended or seriously slighted. So although anger is always a reaction to something, that something may be our thoughts and perceptions.

Anger is an emotional reaction to our perceived needs not being met – and this is potentially a very positive aspect of anger. It is the fact that we feel our needs are not being met which motivates us to intervene and *do* something about it. Anger often drives us either to force someone to meet our needs or to punish them for having failed to meet them. Hopefully they will be less likely to fail us again.

There are three kinds of anger:

- A response to frustration, when our needs are not being met. This could be a need for particular types of food, or enjoyment. Consider a young child's reaction to being thwarted when denied access to sweets at the checkout, or an adolescent whose parents are insisting that they get back in by half past eleven at night. 'Thwarted' is a good word describing the 'causes' of anger, but sometimes it is also the things people do to us that make us angry just as much as being stopped from doing something we feel we have a right to do.

- Anger is sometimes used in quite a calculating way to get what we want. This is called instrumental anger, because we use it as a tool or instrument to achieve something. When children see we are getting angry they may be more likely to obey us, though it may work the other way as well, as, for example, when parents try to avoid confrontations by giving way as soon as a tantrum looms. Children quite quickly learn that the threat of having a tantrum is a very effective way of getting people to back down or to do what they want. Sadly, it is a tactic overused by bullies, whose threat of angry power may frighten us into submission. The anger of the boss is a powerful motivator, which later actually becomes demotivating!

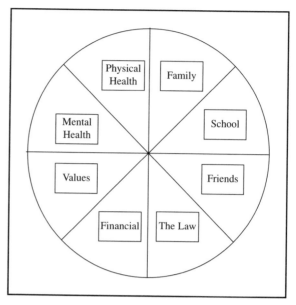

Figure 3.1 *Anger pie*

- Anger is sometimes used as a release of pent-up emotions, particularly when we feel rather powerless to effect change and when the situation seems hopeless. Being at the end of our emotional tether, there is a sense of release when we let our anger out. This is called the cathartic purpose of anger, so that we feel better for having released physical and emotional energy which has been boiling up for some time.

So anger can be a motivator as it can help us achieve our desires or release pent-up frustration. However, 'normal' anger is different from '*problem* anger'. Everybody gets angry to some extent at some things some of the time and that is normal! The essential difference between the two is that 'normal' anger is *constructive*. It lets me know that there is a problem. It tells me that I need to do something about closing the gap between what is and what should be, and it motivates me to think hard and quickly about what I need to do to close the gap. If what I do works, my anger goes. If it does not work, I need to think again. 'Normal' anger solves problems; 'problem anger' creates *more* problems!

Problem anger achieves very short-term gains very effectively, but at the cost of expensive long-term disadvantages or losses. The negative consequences are all long-term; the 'positive' consequences are short-term and often illusory.

Long-term effects of anger

Potter-Effron (1994) describes what he calls our 'personal anger pie'. This pie has eight slices with each slice standing for a 'major area of your life that you have damaged because of your anger'.

Effects on physical health

Anger can be a positive response to feeling threatened – it prepares us to 'fight'. Feeling angry is biologically related to fighting and aggression, just as anxiety is the biological response to another alternative to threat, flight.

Our bodies need to prepare for a sudden expenditure of energy during which significant physiological changes take place. What we all experience when getting very angry includes:

- strange sensations in our stomach

- beads of sweat or perspiration

- tense, tight face and when really angry often quite pale (though we may go red in the face in early stages)

- tense taught muscles, especially legs and arms

- quicker breathing

- heart beating faster

- pupils often dilated

- fidgety small but quick movements

The process of the body preparing for 'flight' is kick-started by the brain sending messages to the adrenal glands to release a chemical called adrenalin into the bloodstream. This triggers the release of glucose which is the fuel the muscles need. But fuel has to be burned to produce energy and for this oxygen is required. That is why breathing becomes more rapid and nostrils flare as the body is taking in air which brings more oxygen into the body. The oxygen is transported by the blood which has to be got round to the muscles very quickly, so the heart pumps much faster, which increases blood pressure. As much oxygen as possible is needed by the muscles, so blood is diverted from where it isn't needed – away from the digestive system (hence the uncomfortable feelings in the stomach and sometimes the feeling of a dry mouth) and away from the face, which may then appear pale. Sweat and perspiration are the body's attempt to cool down the body as it prepares for violent action which will generate lot of heat as the glucose is being burned up. Finally the dilated pupils ensure that vision is as clear and acute as possible to detect small sudden movements of our 'opponent'.

This whole process is fine when we really are preparing for strong physical action as in sport and vigorous leisure pursuits. That is healthy – but anger which is frequent and lasts for long periods is a major health hazard. Too much anger can kill you. As Potter-Effron graphically describes it: 'The angrier you get and stay, the more likely you are to die young. The red face, the clenched fists.

You're like a pressure cooker getting ready to explode. Long term anger can take years off your life.'

He goes on to say that in other senses too, anger is a real health risk – we do violent, uncontrolled things in anger, often hurting ourselves in the process. When windows get broken, fists and wrists often get cut. Road rage frequently ends up with serious injury, or worse, as the care and control we usually exercise go out of the window. People get into actual physical fights when they are very angry as well as possibly becoming very angry with themselves, destroying themselves in 'blind' rage. 'Blind rage' is a telling expression as it derives from the fact that we do not see the serious physical harm we are doing to ourselves.

Effects causing mental ill-health

People who are generally pleasant and friendly can become different people when they become angry. The more often and the longer we remain angry the easier anger seems to become as a 'normal' response. In a sense, it is not unlike a drug, in that there may be short-term 'nice' feelings, but with potentially long-term disastrous consequences. Like drugs, tolerance levels change with usage. The more angry we become, the easier it is to become angry – and smaller and smaller slights and frustrations elicit the same or even greater amounts of anger. It can grow and fester to the extent that all the world appears hostile and frustrating, so that anger becomes a habit leading to irrational antisocial behaviour which becomes 'a conduct disorder'.

The after-effects of severe angry outbursts or rages are emotionally unpleasant. The release of the brain chemicals adrenalin and noradrenalin in angry outbursts leaves us feeling emotionally flat and empty, often depressed and guilty. In such a state, we are easily irritated and hypersensitive to wrongs and hurts and the whole process can easily start all over again.

Effects on family life

Angry parents often have angry children – and angry children produce angry parents. There is plenty of evidence too that parents who use angry outbursts and accompanying aggression to control their children play a very significant part in the development of antisocial and delinquent children. Parents who model ways of angrily exerting control over other people are readily imitated by their children, leading to a coercive style of interaction between members of the family, as Gerry Patterson (1986) has convincingly shown. Such families are fraught with tensions, squabbles and fights, with a cycle of bullying and being bullied. Long-term anger destroys effective family life which is about love and concern, not about fighting and scapegoating.

What about the effects of angry children on family life? Much depends upon how parents cope with their children's anger. We have seen how feelings of anger are related to being thwarted. The reality is that consciously or unconsciously parents will never meet all the needs of their children. For some psychologists the fact of being a child inevitably means that there will be loving and hating feelings experienced towards parents. How parents handle the expression of such feelings may prove crucial to subsequent adjustment and mental health. Children need to feel that their 'uncontrollable rage' is actually contained – the last thing they need is the parent who buckles in weakness and abrogates control in the presence of childhood anger. There are two extremes to avoid – one, matching the child's anger with your own rage, and the other, allowing the child to feel omnipotent and all powerful by using anger and threats of anger as a way of control.

Anger, when it becomes a dominant and frequent emotion within families, is pernicious and destructive of all that families stand for. Sadly, angry families are often characterised by the likelihood of serious physical or emotional child abuse, or both.

Effects on friends and friendships

How children get on with others is increasingly recognised as a good predictor of how well they will do at school, at work and ultimately for the quality of their physical and mental health. Very young nursery age children who show a lack of emotional control that leads to aggression to their peers are now known to be at severe risk of forming poor peer relationships at junior and into secondary schooling and are at greater risk of delinquency and poor academic attainments generally. Clearly a lack of anger control and the stability of friendships are mutually incompatible. Friendship is about trust, sharing and concern and these qualities are poorly developed in people who can not control their angry feelings. Angry children ruin friendships, and friendships are needed for a satisfying and fulfilling life.

Effects on schooling

School is the place where issues of authority and peer relationships come together in the lives of children. Classrooms should be places where children learn together and where, even more than in the family, issues of 'fairness' are very high on the agenda. Angry people are extremely sensitive to perceived unfairness and it is 'authority' which thwarts them from getting what they think they have rights to. Angry children pose major problems to classroom management, because being very angry is to become 'out of control' – and that is a teacher's nightmare.

One of the reasons why angry children tend to not do well at school is that the teaching relationship is threatened when learners do not attend and do not cooperate. This requires a focus on the teacher and the teacher's agenda. Angry children get caught up only in their own agenda and this threatens the teacher–learner relationship – and therefore they do not learn very effectively. Angry children are likely to be educational underachievers.

Finally, because the classroom is essentially a learning group, angry children disrupt the learning of other children as well as their own. Children learn best in a secure and fairly predictable environment. Angry outbursts lead to behaviours which are predictable only in their unpredictability.

Effects of anger and the law

The relationship with anger and delinquency is clear. Many serious crimes such as physical assault, murder, and criminal damage are done in anger. Alcohol and drugs reduce the levels of rational control and encourage angry reactions. Angry children are perhaps less likely to become involved directly in criminal proceedings than adults, but there is strong evidence that angry children are very likely to become angry adults.

Children who are angrily threatening the security of teachers and classmates make up the vast proportion of the increasing numbers of pupils being excluded from schools, now running at some 13,000 children permanently excluded annually. The consequences of exclusion are severe in both the short and long term. If not actually excluded, angry students are much more likely to be referred for formal assessment of their special educational needs for emotional and behavioural difficulties (EBD). This is the major area in which 'inclusion' policies are currently not working well. In the current climate there is very little likelihood of reduction in the number of places in special schools for pupils in EBD. Without entering into wider issues of special educational provision, there are certainly disadvantages in a child having to attend a special school on the grounds that they pose a threat to other children if they remain in a mainstream school. Such children tend to lose out in terms of the breadth of the curriculum available to them and in the absence of normal role models.

Effects on the general quality of life

Angry people are, by definition, unhappy and discontented people whose self-esteem is very low. The way we value ourselves is the measure by which we are able to value others. The more that children believe themselves to be of unique value, because of what they are, rather than because of what they do, the less likely they are to feel the need to put other children down in order to defend their own sense of worth. Our ability to manage anger has long-term effects on the values we hold, on the way we construe our part in the community and our ability to sustain meaningful and fulfilling relationships.

Financial effects of anger

Angry people are very expensive! In violent rages, children stamp on computers, throw books and bricks at windows, destroy furniture. Arson of whole schools may be related to issues of anger management. Repairing this damage costs money.

People get damaged as well. The Friday and Saturday night overflowing casualty departments and the treatment of injuries inflicted in anger drain the National Health Service of scarce resources. Many of these casualties are youngsters. Special school placements are extremely expensive and those for angry young people, those with acting out challenging behaviour, are sometimes the most expensive of all. A figure of £50,000 per annum for a single child is not uncommon. Surely we should be using these scarce resources more effectively?

Having considered what anger does to us we will go on to examine what we do with anger and distinguish between effective and problem anger.

Summary

- Anger is part of the 'fight' response to perceived threat.

- There are three major functions of anger:

    a response to frustration

    a way of getting what we want

    a release of pent-up emotions

- 'Problem anger' has major long-term effects on:

    our physical and mental health

    family life and friendship

    success in school

    involvement with the law

    personal and social financial costs

Action

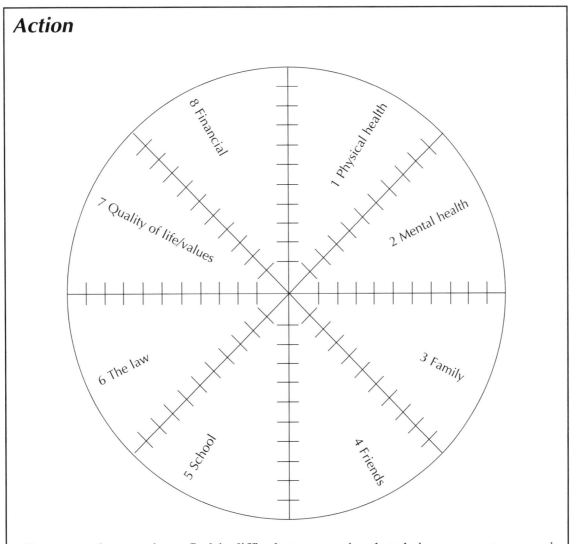

Young people sometimes find it difficult to recognise that their response to anger is causing problems. Help them to identify areas in which to set goals for themselves by rating how anger is affecting their satisfaction in each section of the Anger Pie for 1 to 10. A score of 10 (on the edge of the circle) means anger is not affecting anything in this part of their life, whilst a score of 1 (at the centre of the circle) means that this area is being very badly affected by their anger. Join up the scores and you will see where things are a little wobbly!

Chapter 4

What do we do with anger?

In this chapter we will look at what we can do with anger, both when we get angry ourselves and when others are angry with us. The way in which we deal with our own anger is likely to be reflected in the way we deal with other people's anger.

Factors affecting what we do with anger

What we do with anger will depend on the combination of a number of factors:

- learned responses

- belief systems

- unconscious motivators

- individual differences

Learned responses

Which process is considered to be the primary factor will depend on your favoured psychological perspective as discussed in Chapter 2. In this chapter an interactionist approach is assumed, with all factors contributing in a greater or lesser extent to the behaviour we see.

We learn how to express emotions from observing our carers and by learning behaviours that have 'worked for us' in the past. The responses we learned will have enabled us to get our own needs met, albeit this may only be in the short term. Experiences that we encounter when we are babies and young children will be those that we have internalised and subsequently express in our behaviour patterns. Thus, our early experiences of how others deal with anger and how our expressions of anger have been responded to, will have a significant effect on how we respond later to our own and others' anger.

Belief systems

The notion that our own internal thoughts and perceptions also affect our responses was introduced in Chapter 2. A cognitive approach to explaining behaviour, Rational Emotive Therapy (founded by Albert Ellis), suggests that it is not the events themselves that make us angry, but how we think about them. Thus, in the firework analogy described in Chapter 1, our own thoughts and beliefs form part of the lighted fuse. A teacher tells a pupil how well he's doing with a piece of work and the pupil 'explodes', tearing his work to shreds and throwing it in the bin. Anger is viewed as a response to threat in this book: that threat can be to our sense of self, our self-esteem and the way in which we view ourselves, as well as to more tangible things such as getting our own way, our possessions or personal safety. In the example given above, one possible explanation might be that the pupil is disappointed with his own level of work, wishes he could do better and therefore when the teacher expresses pleasure at the work, it threatens the pupil's view of himself as more able than he is demonstrating: '*If the teacher thinks this is good work for me, they must think I am not capable of doing better*'. This internal perception results in an angry outburst which appears inappropriate and unjust to the teacher who has been trying to encourage the pupil by giving praise and being positive.

Unconscious motivators

The psychodynamic theory of psychology outlined in Chapter 2 (Freud), give us an alternative way to consider underlying causes of angry outbursts. Within this model it would be considered that our responses may be motivated by unconscious desires and fears that we are unaware of at the time. For example, a child may have been separated from a parent or carer at an early age through death, illness, or family breakdown and may be fearful of forming close relationships for fear of being 'rejected' again. In this instance, the pupil at school may appear to be deliberately picking fights with adults in order to test out the relationship or stop the relationship developing to the point at which the child would be hurt by another loss. These will be unconscious fears, inaccessible to the pupil themselves. Discussing with a pupil 'why' they have been so angry is therefore unlikely to help you get to the root cause in this instance and may account for those times when you find yourself thinking that the pupil's behaviour is completely unpredictable, with no obvious triggers setting the fuse.

Individual differences

Recent biological research indicates that individuals have predispositions for experiencing emotions to a greater or lesser extent that are rooted in biology (Gardner 1993, LeDoux 1994).

Emotional reactions are directed by a part of the brain called the amygdala and can bypass the thinking, conscious part of the brain, called the neo-cortex. The person who appears to have difficulty identifying their own feelings and putting them into words would therefore show different underlying neurological patterns to the person who appears emotionally sensitive and volatile. As many of our emotional reactions happen out of awareness, those people who are self aware to a greater extent will find it easier to control their emotions as this gives more opportunities for monitoring their responses and considering whether or not they are helpful in the long term. A high level of self-awareness is therefore likely to be associated with healthy expression of emotions.

Other individual factors which affect our ability to respond in a controlled, rational way, rather than in an uncontrolled irrational manner, include physical health, stress, relationships, work, etc. The way we deal with and respond to these external factors will however be dependent on the internal factors mentioned above.

What we do with our own anger

We may deal with our own anger in one or more of the following ways:

- displacement

- repression

- suppression

- express it ineffectively (problem anger)

- express it effectively (normal anger)

We will look at each of these in turn.

Displaced anger

Anger may be displaced onto a person or object that is not the focus of the anger itself. This is usually because it is considered unsafe to be angry with the real focus of the anger. For example, a pupil who has been in trouble at home in the morning, may feel unable to express their anger at home for fear of making things worse, or even risking physical or emotional abuse. It may well be that this is displaced onto a tutor, or class teacher, when the pupil gets to school. In the short term this may leave the pupil feeling better due to a release of physical and emotional tension which has been simmering for some time. In the long term however, it is likely to spoil relationships at school, hamper effective learning, and damage self-esteem, leaving the pupil feeling guilty and depressed after the event. Neither does it go any way to resolving the conflict that has arisen at home, thereby increasing the probability that the behaviour patterns will continue at home as well as creating a second range of problems at school.

Repressed anger

The term repression comes from psychodynamic theories of psychology as introduced when discussing unconscious motivators. The unconscious part of the mind is assumed to be able to store memories and control behaviour and feelings, without it coming into our conscious awareness. Repressed anger is then anger which is affecting our behaviour but of which we are unaware. To understand causes of angry outbursts in this instance, we would have to help the individual bring the unconscious memories and feelings into conscious awareness.

Suppressed anger

Suppressed anger refers to anger which we are consciously aware of, but that is not expressed by choice. We may have learnt at a very young age that to show anger is 'naughty' or 'bad'. In fact demonstrating negative feelings at all may be considered inappropriate in some families and cultures. Imagine the scenario in which a young child is given a present from the Christmas bran tub at school, which she does not like. It is likely that the child will be encouraged to express pleasure and to say thank you, irrespective of her true feelings. We are usually encouraged to suppress strong feelings which may hurt others. However, it is likely that we deliver confusing and inconsistent messages when we do not find a way of expressing our feelings accurately. If there is a mismatch between verbal and non-verbal messages it is the non-verbal messages that will be the most powerful. It is therefore important that we learn appropriate ways to express our feelings, which respect the feelings and points of view of others. Although we would not be expecting a young child to have an angry outburst on receiving an unwanted present, as this would clearly upset others' feelings and devalue the act of giving, it would be important for the child to learn appropriate language and times to express their disappointment in a healthy and positive way.

Suppression of anger may be a way of trying to avoid hurting those we care about, and stems from learning that to express strong negative feelings is unacceptable. This is likely to have been learnt when we are young, so that guilt will be a strong inhibitor for the appropriate expression of anger. Unfortunately strong feelings that are not expressed may build up until they 'leak' out onto unimportant matters, or until they 'explode' inappropriately, hurting those we care about more deeply than the original conflict would have done.

There is a view that is widely held that suppressed and repressed anger may be the cause of depression in some instances. Depression is seen as anger turned inwards onto the individual themselves rather than outward onto the appropriate focus. This can become a deeply entrenched way of behaving, having built up throughout the formative years. Culturally, women seem to be more at risk of guilt when feeling strong negative emotions, as girls are more likely than boys to be taught to be compliant, and to be the peacemakers in the family. These attitudes heighten the probability of anger being repressed, suppressed or focused inwardly, so that the person feels that it is they who are 'bad' rather than that they are angry at events outside themselves.

Expressing anger ineffectively (problem anger)

Anger expressed ineffectively is likely to be out of rational control and lead to damaged relationships and negative physiological effects. We are all familiar with the feeling that we regret having said or done something in 'the heat of the moment'. Strong emotions can be expressed destructively and lead to confusion and hurt and get us nowhere in terms of meeting our own or others' needs.

Problem anger is expressed in a hostile, aggressive way and may take the form of a violent outburst involving both verbal and physical aggression. Verbally, we will be condemning the other person totally, labelling them as 'bad' and overstating the case: for example, 'You're completely useless, you never do as I ask'; 'I'll never be able to trust you again'; 'You're so naughty, I simply can't stand any more.' In the short term this explosive expression of anger may feel subjectively quite good, as it releases tension, gives a feeling of power and sometimes may get you what you want (but at a cost). Long-term however, it is likely to damage relationships and escalate hostility within them.

Our belief systems not only affect what triggers anger, but also influences how we become irrational and inaccurate as a result of the escalation of anger and aggression. We are more likely to think that the other person involved had deliberate intentions to threaten us in some way and to overestimate the extent of this. We also become unable to see things from other perspectives and cannot begin to consider the other person's point of view.

Our ability for rational thinking disappears when we lose our temper, and we also suffer the physiological consequences of aggressive behaviour as discussed in Chapter 3 'What does anger do to you?'. This combined with the feeling of having lost control will leave us feeling depressed and low. It will also leave us with an unresolved conflict, for conciliation becomes difficult and unlikely when we are on the receiving end of an aggressive outburst. Behaviours may change initially through fear of engendering more aggression, but there is unlikely to be any genuine resolution of conflict. Hostility may then take the form of undermining the other person behind their back and getting others on your side (plotting revenge!), thus escalating the difficulties and making successful communication extremely difficult.

Anger expressed effectively (normal anger)

When anger is expressed effectively, it provides an opportunity for learning and change. The positive resolution of conflict can lead to improvements in relationships and situations that would otherwise remain unsatisfactory to all parties. Anger can be expressed in such a way as to respect other people's feelings and points of view, even when differing from one's own. In this way the expression of anger becomes a positive act.

Expressing anger effectively involves communicating the concerns we have whilst still respecting the other person's right to have alternative views. This quotation from Voltaire (from Dryden 1996) sums up the position well: 'I disapprove of what you say, but I will defend to the death your right to say it.' We need to learn to be able to express strong feelings without attacking the other person as an individual, by dealing with the particular behaviour that is upsetting us. Feelings can be communicated without blaming the other person, and changes in behaviour can be requested positively. In this way, our own goals can be pursued whilst still respecting the other person.

Having considered what anger is, what it does, and how we use it, we are now going to build on our understanding by using the metaphor of a storm to characterise the processes involved.

Summary

What we do with anger will depend on:

- learned responses

- belief systems

- unconscious motivators

- individual differences

We may deal with our own anger in one of the following ways:

- displacement

- repression

- suppression

- ineffective expression (problem anger)

- effective expression (normal anger)

Action

Consider your own style of anger by completing the following checklist:

When I am angry, I (tick one box for each response)

	Often (a)	Sometimes (b)	Rarely (c)	Never (d)
1. Become cold and overly controlled	☐	☐	☐	☐
2. Shout loudly	☐	☐	☐	☐
3. Cry	☐	☐	☐	☐
4. Completely lose control	☐	☐	☐	☐
5. Use verbal abuse	☐	☐	☐	☐
6. Become physically aggressive	☐	☐	☐	☐
7. Ignore it but find myself angry about something 'safe'	☐	☐	☐	☐
8. Walk away	☐	☐	☐	☐
9. Damage property	☐	☐	☐	☐
10. Hope it will go away	☐	☐	☐	☐

Score your responses by putting a circle round a number, depending on whether you ticked a, b, c, d.

	(a)	(b)	(c)	(d)
1.	1	2	3	4
2.	4	3	2	1
3.	1	2	3	4
4.	4	3	2	1
5.	4	3	2	1
6.	4	3	2	1
7.	1	2	3	4
8.	1	2	3	4
9.	4	3	2	1
10.	1	2	3	4

Add up your score. Scores between 31 and 40 suggest that your own responses to anger may be ineffective as they lack control. Responses between 10 and 19 suggest that your responses may be suppressed or repressed. They do not lack control but may lead to 'leaked feelings' and are unlikely to be helpful in getting your needs met. Responses in the middle range suggest that your style of anger is well-balanced.

Because this scale has not been 'normed' on a large sample the scores should be interpreted cautiously.

SECTION TWO

THE STORM

Chapter 5

Planning to avoid a storm

Storms have a number of defining elements but are a natural feature of the environment and part of a system of global weather patterns. So it is then that a brief cloudburst even of small proportions is linked to a bigger set of environmental factors. Similarly, a child having a brief but troubling tantrum has an effect on and is affected by numerous environmental factors. This is well described by Bronfenbrenner's Ecological Model of Development shown as Figure 5.1 as a kind of 'gob-stopper', with the child at the centre influenced by a host of surrounding environmental factors. These factors include the immediate or local influences such as the child's immediate nuclear family and the school, and may also include other close influences such as friends, health services, the church, and local community. Beyond them are more distant but potentially important influences such as the extended family, neighbours, the media, school governors and the local education authority, and social services.

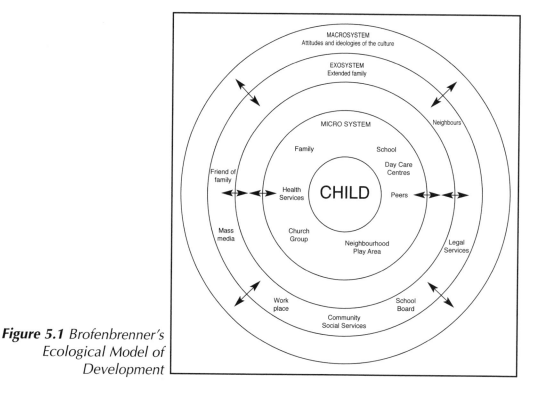

Figure 5.1 *Brofenbrenner's Ecological Model of Development*

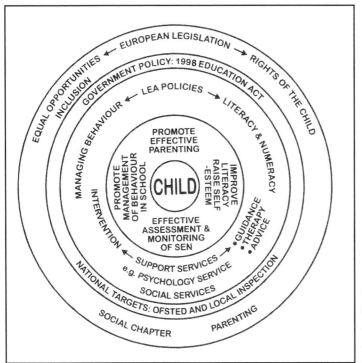

Figure 5.2 Promoting school effectiveness. © Southampton Psychology Service/ISIS. Adapted from Brofenbrenner's Ecological Model of Development

Figures 5.1 and 5.2 show how complex interrelationships between many factors may influence a child. 'Within-child' factors will also influence how they respond to the environment. Bronfenbrenner's model may be adapted to focus more closely on the factors affecting children's education, which in turn will be linked to the way they manage their anger.

This chapter will look at only some of the elements referred to above and in Figures 5.1 and 5.2, and is concerned principally with planning to avoid a storm at school. Children's anger is often less tolerated at school, if only because institutions are frequently more formal than families and have rules and an ethos managed by more people.

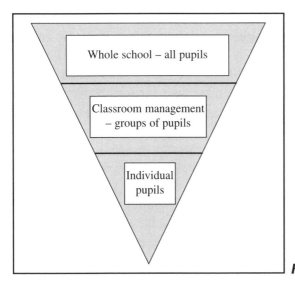

Figure 5.3 Three levels for managing anger

There are three levels at which children's anger management may be considered and these are depicted diagramatically as Figure 5.3. This shows that managing anger, in common with managing behaviour, can be tackled at three levels:

- whole school

- classroom/group level

- individual pupil level

Whole-school factors

A school staff that takes the trouble to work out a set of policies all underpinned by an explicit belief in the maximum possible development of every child, will have at least one policy covering positive management of behaviour within a caring and humane framework.

Many teachers and governors complain that policies are simply pieces of paper produced to satisfy OFSTED, and the same teachers argue that the element of 'wheel reinvention' resulting from the development of these policies in every school is a waste of energy. The combined experience of the authors over many years of working in schools suggests the reverse. Primarily the ownership of a policy is fostered by the involvement of as many staff and other members of the community as possible, and this is further enhanced when the school staff have worked hard to develop a mission with clear aims and objectives all being pursued within a positive ethos. Schools without such a plan will invariably be poor at managing anger, and will be characterised by high exclusion rates and poor classroom management skills.

Four main components of a good policy will comprise, firstly the *whole-school environment*, which includes the physical curricular, and social environment. This complex set of whole-school environmental factors requires schools to actively consider how to optimise school management style, relationships between teachers, pupils and teachers as well as other staff, school staff and parents, and staff relationships to other agencies. The betterment of the physical environment, even on a tight budget, is likely to have a positive impact on how both children and staff behave. For example, the use of carpets and other soft furnishing significantly reduces noise levels and humanises the school setting, which in turn tends to improve behaviour.

Secondly, the policy requires the establishment of a range of *rewards and sanctions* all aimed at encouraging appropriate and discouraging inappropriate behaviour. Rewards need to be age-appropriate, predictable, valued, ethically sound, and are best given for a variety of reasons covering effort, achievement, appropriate conformity, and courtesy. Similar parameters for sanctions or consequences are needed, but the reasons for giving them need to be fully transparent and well understood by staff, governors, pupils and parents in order to head-off unnecessary confrontation.

Thirdly, the policy needs to have an emphasis on *teaching new behaviours*, which may come through a variety of cross-curricular themes as part of personal, social, and health education. Having an active programme of social skills training, and running anger management groups should be given serious consideration. This may require support from outside agencies such as the educational psychology service, particularly in the development phase of these practices.

Fourthly, the policy needs to explicitly address the school's approach to *handling crises*, which will inevitably occur even in a very well run school. There should be robust contingency plans for dealing with fights, bullying, vandalism, verbal abuse and generally disruptive behaviour. The arrangements for dealing with any of these events should be known to staff, governors, pupils and parents and be consistent with ethical and professional practices.

Very few behaviour policies drawn up by schools currently address the issue of anger, and many simply expect children to conform and have no explicit strategies for either reacting effectively, or better still, teaching children how they might better manage their anger at school.

If each of the four components described above is covered well, the policy is highly likely to lead to the school being both efficient and effective, irrespective of whether it is pupils, parents, staff, or OFSTED doing the evaluation. In a fascinating study, *Success Against The Odds: Effective Schools in Disadvantaged Areas*, by the National Commission on Education (1996), there are ten features of success listed, and these are summarised below since they are also highly likely to be features of schools with excellent management of behaviour. At first sight many of these factors appear only distantly related to anger management, but in practice a school could use each of these as headings to design part of their anger management strategy.

1. Strong leadership by the head in identifying anger management as a priority component of a behaviour policy.

2. Good atmosphere from shared values and attractive environment – for example, values concerning anger management.

3. High expectations of pupils, in terms of effective anger management.

4. Clear focus on teaching and learning of anger management strategies for teachers and pupils to use.

5. Good assessment of pupils.

6. Pupils share responsibility for learning.

7. Pupils participate in the life of the school.

8. Incentives for pupils to succeed.

9. Parental involvement.

10. Extracurricular activities to broaden pupils' interests and build good relationships in school.

Classroom and group management

In addition to the whole-school factors discussed above, consideration needs to be given specifically to a school-wide class or group management model that promotes an approach to anger management that features:

- *Consistency* – both of practice within and between teachers and other staff, which further means that rules, rewards and sanctions all need to be relevant, reasonable and implemented by everyone using broadly agreed criteria.

- *High expectations of behaviour and achievement* – which need to be matched by a reward system that has equal access for all, irrespective of ability. Rewards need to be real, appropriate, relatively immediate and delivered in a way that makes it possible to receive them (for some youngsters this may be non-public and subtle, as they have difficulty coping with praise after years of not getting any). Class-wide reinforcement is also a powerful motivator, and can be used to turn round the behaviour of some very angry children if they are given a real opportunity to support the class achieving a goal.

- *Cohesiveness* – so that a pro-social atmosphere is created by staff being fair and holding to agreed values made explicit to children, parents and each other.

- *Constancy* – in as much as the classroom environment should be relatively predictable and changes made gradually in an evolutionary way wherever possible.

- *Satisfaction* – both for teachers and learners, and most likely to be achieved by differentiation of work to a level that puts success within the grasp of every pupil most, if not all, of the time.

The school-wide class or group management model should also aim to reduce:

- *Competition* – which may be unhealthy if it is based on a need simply to outperform a less able peer, and consequently divert energy from the pursuit of individual excellence within a climate of mutual respect.

- *Confrontation* – between adults and children should generally be avoided in open classroom, and guidelines on how to do this are described in Chapter 8.

Summary

Planning to avoid a storm involves:

- an understanding of the wider system affecting the behaviour of children and young people

- an analysis of the relative contribution of factors which are

    – within child

    – within teacher

    – within parent

    – within school

    – within community

    – within society

- helping a school to construct a policy which is sophisticated, effective, and fair; preventative approaches require a school to formulate, implement and review policies which cover the

    – whole school – classroom or groups

    – the individual

Action

Schools need to consider the following factors when drafting a positive behaviour management policy.

1. Who is contributing to policy formulation?
   staff   *governors*   *parents*   *pupils*   *other agencies*

2. What are the school's
   aims   *values*   *ethos?*

3. Whose behaviour do we mean?
   pupils   *teachers*   *parents*   *other staff*   *visitors*

4. What are the school rules?
   implicit   *explicit*   *widely known?*

5. How is appropriate behaviour encouraged?
   parents   *praise*   *rewards*   *celebrations*

6. How is inappropriate behaviour discouraged?
   parents   *consequences*   *sanctions*   *recording reparation*

7. Are there explicit criteria for the use of sanctions?
   detention   *tasks*   *parents called*   *exclusion*

8. How is bullying dealt with?
   policy   *no blame*   *parental involvement*
                     approach

9. How is self-discipline encouraged?
   relationships   openness   *trust*   *choice*

10. How is self-esteem promoted?
    language   *rewards*   *programmes*   *monitoring*

11. How are staff supported?
    training   *peers*   *management*   *other agencies*

12. How are policies made fair?
    age   *gender*   *race*   *special needs*

13. How are policies evaluated?
    review   *revision*   *training*   *resources*

Having answered these questions a school will have identified current strengths and weaknesses in their positive behaviour management policy, and can then proceed to develop it more effectively.

Chapter 6

Weathering the storm

Even if a school has a good behaviour policy which incorporates effective anger management strategies, they will still have occasional storms.

In this chapter we will look at how to minimise the difficulties involved when someone responds to an angry outburst that looks as if it may escalate into an aggressive incident. We are discussing problem anger in this chapter, anger that is expressed ineffectively and is likely to endanger relationships or safety. It could include either physical attack which is directed at people or property, or verbal attack, which is personally condemning or abusive. We will consider the most effective time at which to intervene, the importance of early warning signs and some defusing strategies.

The stages involved in an aggressive incident can help us to understand how and when to intervene effectively and also how our own reactions will affect the direction of the incident. The Assault Cycle (as described in Breakwell 1997) has five stages of phases:

The Assault Cycle

- the trigger stage

- the escalation stage

- the crisis stage

- the plateau or recovery stage

- the post-crisis depression stage

The *trigger* stage can be related to the firework model described in Chapter 1, and is an event that 'ignites' a person's fuse, so stimulating thoughts and feelings that lead to problem anger. It is the stage at which a pupil perceives an incident or event as threatening. This can include threats to self-esteem and self-image as well as the more tangible threats to personal safety or property. The best time to intervene with young people is at the very early stage, as the body has not yet become fully aroused physiologically, and they are not so fired up as to be incapable of listening or responding to others. Once the body gets prepared for 'fight or flight', and they are reaching the explosion point in the firework

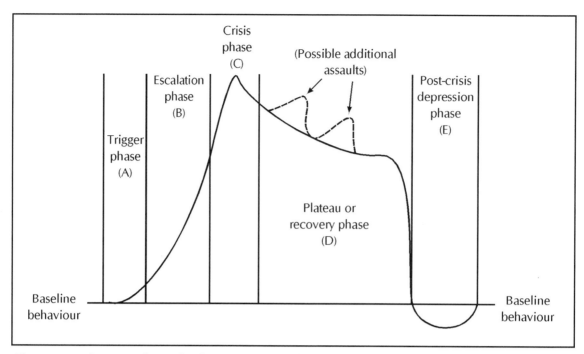

Figure 6.1 *The Assault Cycle (from* Coping with Aggressive Behaviour, *Breakwell 1997)*

analogy, it is very much harder to change the course of events. We are then talking about managing a crisis which is discussed in Chapter 9.

The *escalation* stage is the time at which the body is preparing itself physiologically for 'fight or flight'. Adrenaline is released into the body, the muscles tense, breathing becomes rapid and blood pressure rises. There may be some chance of changing behaviour at this stage, but it is becoming increasingly unlikely as the person will be less able to make rational judgements as the arousal increases. This could be likened to the fuse of the firework and as such will be shorter or longer depending on individual differences. These will be the result of early learning experiences of how others dealt with anger and how our expressions of anger have been responded to, and individual biological predispositions, as discussed in Chapter 4.

The *crisis* stage is the stage at which the pupil is completely unable to make rational judgements or to demonstrate any empathy with others. This will be the firework exploding in our analogy. It is very difficult for people to listen to others or understand what is being said to them at this stage.

The explosion or outburst is followed by the *plateau/recovery* stage during which the anger begins to subside. It takes time for the body to return to normal. During this stage it is easy to escalate the anger again by intervening inappropriately. The body is still partly prepared for action and the feelings that accompany this stage are likely to leave the person feeling vulnerable and confused. It is possible that guilty feelings will start to show through, and that these may in themselves feel threatening to a young person and escalate the angry outburst again.

The *post-crisis/depression* stage is the phase in which the body needs to rest and recover from the high state of arousal that it has been in. The ability to listen and think clearly begins to return at this stage and it is likely that the pupil will begin to feel unhappy about the incident that has just occurred. Guilt often leads to negative feelings about oneself , but it is helpful to make a distinction between guilty feelings about yourself and remorse about the behaviour. Guilt directed at oneself can be perceived as negative as it is likely to reduce self-esteem and make the young person feel bad about themselves. Remorse for the behaviour could lead to effective responses such as apologising, making amends, or thinking carefully about how to change the behaviour in the future.

It is important to be aware that the assault cycle can easily be sparked off again if the fuse is re-lit in the recovery phase. We often underestimate how long the last two stages of the assault cycle take and so intervene before the other person has fully recovered. In adults it can take up to 90 minutes after a serious outburst for the body to return to normal levels. If two individuals are involved in an argument it is possible that they will continue to trigger each other and so repeat the assault cycle for some time. In practice it is sensible to leave at least 45 minutes, and ideally one hour, before a teacher or parent discusses a major incident with the young person involved. The amount of time needed for the person to unwind will depend on the age of the child and the severity of the incident. Young children are much quicker to recover from strong feelings and are likely to be feeling fine whilst the adult is left feeling drained and uncomfortable.

Early warning signs

There is often an opportunity to stop anger developing into an outburst if you learn to identify the early warning signs of difficult behaviours. This will depend on knowing the pupil well and will take time to learn, but the earlier we can intervene the better.

Intervening in the early stages of an outburst stands a much better chance of averting a crisis than leaving things to develop. This is where identifying early warning signs could be helpful in reducing the likelihood of things escalating. Any techniques which distract or divert the young person's attention from their own distress should be helpful. Alternatively activities which help the person to relax and discussion and negotiation may be effective. Because we, the adults, are likely to feel threatened by the potential outburst that we perceive, we must be aware that our reactions are likely to mirror the assault cycle as well. It is important that we do not escalate the outburst at this stage by getting angry too. It will help us to stay calm if we are able to distance ourselves from the incident. Even if

Figure 6.2 *Early warning signs*

the anger appears to be directed personally at us, it is important to be aware that it is also a reflection of the child's internal conflicts and difficulties, and may in part result from strategies that the young person has learnt to cope with problems or gain attention.

Early warning signs can include any of the following:

- physical agitation – pacing up and down, fiddling with equipment, twitching legs

- change in facial expression

- change in eye contact

- change in body posture

- change in facial colouring

- change in tone of voice

- verbal challenges

- change of position in the classroom

- rapid mood swings

- over sensitivity to suggestions or criticisms.

It is important to stress that these 'signs' will be individual to each child and that knowing the child well is important. Basically the signs we are looking for will involve a change in behaviour representing a heightened state of arousal. There may be few signs and you may need to look hard to find them. They may also vary according to the environment and the nature of the perceived threat.

At this stage adults often feel in a dilemma between ignoring the signs and hoping the problem will go away, and intervening inappropriately and escalating the behaviours. Ignoring signs of aggressive outbursts is unhelpful as this is the beginning of an anger reaction that has a momentum of its own once it is in full flight. Some positive action from the adult is necessary. Phrases that are likely to make matters worse at this stage include anything that devalues the other person, for example,

'Pull yourself together'

'I thought you were more grown up than this'

'Don't be silly'

'Now don't start that!'

Finding appropriate ways to intervene at this stage is one of the best ways to avoid aggressive confrontations.

The following strategies may help to defuse the anger and reduce physiological arousal:

Defusing techniques

- *Distraction* – This is more likely to be effective with younger children. Distracting with a favourite toy or an event happening elsewhere may be enough to divert their attention away from their own distress.

- *Relocation* – By removing the pupil from the environment that is stressful, we may avert the escalation of the outburst. For example pupils can be sent on an errand of responsibility. This has the advantage of supporting self-esteem as well as removing them from the difficult situation. It may be that you would feel that you would want to go with the pupil if you were concerned for their safety or felt that they may need added strategies to support them. Conversely, if the anger is directed at you, it may be advantageous to allow 'cool off' time without you present. Clearly it is important that whole-school systems are in place in order that there are agreed procedures for such eventualities.

- *Change of activity* – It may be sufficient to alter the task that you are asking the child to participate in. It will be important that a

Figure 6.3 *How might the storm be prevented?*

positive behaviour programme incorporates strategies to help the pupil learn how to deal with tasks that they find threatening.

- *Physical proximity* – Some children respond well to physical closeness. Eye contact, minimal physical touch, may also be helpful. It is important to know the person well in order to know whether this approach will be successful or not. For some pupils this may add to their feelings of threat and insecurity. This strategy should be avoided when working with pupils you do not know well.

- *Humour* – This is also a strategy to be used with caution as the pupil could misinterpret it as belittling their response. Certainly sarcasm and irony should be avoided. Although it is high risk, humour can be extremely successful as the physiological responses involved in humour are the exact opposite to those of anger. Laughter is therefore a very good antidote to anger.

- *Communication* – For young people it is important to feel that they are being listened to effectively and that their opinions are being valued. This encourages feelings of being in control, which is particularly important for teenagers. It may be that this is not an appropriate time for in depth discussions about anxieties and feelings but reassuring a pupil that there will be an opportunity for further discussion at a later time is important. Follow up work from the incident should be several hours after the incident, following which a fresh start can be made.

- *Relaxation* – In order to reduce the physiological arousal that accompanies the build up of anger, it may be appropriate to encourage the pupil to employ direct relaxation techniques, including deep breathing, tensing and untensing muscles. Clearly these techniques will have to be taught at a time when the pupil is calm and responsive and then reminders given when the early warning signs are noticed. It may be that a pupil needs to release some of the pent up feelings and reduce physiological arousal by taking part in something physically active such as running or kicking a football. Others find music very relaxing and there may be ways to allow pupils to either play or listen to music to help them to relax.

It is important to remember that when we feel under a perceived threat we are likely to become physiologically aroused and risk entering the assault cycle ourselves. If we do that we are far more likely to feel punitive and to get into a power struggle with the young person that will escalate rather than defuse the situation. We must, therefore, be able to keep ourselves calm both psychologically and physically. Earlier we suggested that depersonalising the incident is helpful in remaining psychologically calm. The relaxation, distraction and defusing strategies recommended for the pupil may well be helpful for the adult as well as in avoiding the incident becoming confrontational.

Another issue that causes concern at this stage is whether or not we are reinforcing unacceptable behaviour by providing 'pleasant' alternatives. For example, if a young person shows signs of an aggressive outburst when asked to conform to a school rule, and he or she is offered alternatives when the early warning signs of aggression are spotted, are we encouraging that person to flaunt the rules in future? It is important to separate the issues of avoiding an aggressive outburst and teaching a pupil to choose more appropriate ways to behave. A positive behaviour programme must always be in place to teach the pupil to understand the triggers of the outbursts and to make alternative choices when he or she feels threatened or upset. The consequences of problem anger however, are so significant that it is important to help the pupil to avoid the outburst at the point at which the fuse has been lit. Understanding and avoiding triggers which light the fuse will be an important part of the pupil's positive behaviour programme.

The nature of the strategies suggested for defusing difficult situations make it important that a complete plan is in place for pupils who exhibit aggressive outbursts. This plan must consider what strategies to employ at the point of conflict as well as positive behaviour strategies to teach the pupil how to make better choices. Clearly a whole-school approach will be needed to support individual strategies employed, and when the storm subsides there is still work to be done and this is the subject of the next chapter.

Summary

This chapter considers when teachers or carers can effectively intervene by considering:

- the assault cycle

- early warning signs

- defusing strategies

Action

Working with a pupil that you know well, spend some time observing their behaviour in order to identify three early warning signs of an angry outburst.

Early warning signs

1.

2.

3.

In order to intervene at the trigger stage, identify three defusing strategies that you would like to try when you see the early warning signs.

Defusing strategies

1.

2.

3.

Log your attempts and the results.

Chapter 7

After the storm

A violent storm is the result of intense electrical energy – just as an angry emotional outburst is the result of intense and high levels of physiological arousal. Storms pass over, but they frequently rumble on in the distance and we can sometimes get caught out when they suddenly return. The 'assault cycle' we have considered earlier reminds us that we have to make sure that we do not misjudge the

Figure 7.1 *After the raging storm comes . . .*

levels of arousal and so provoke another outburst. In working with pupils who have become very angry, and particularly if this anger has been expressed violently, we need to remember a very important principle: that the higher the level of arousal, the less rational that person is likely to be. There is simply no point in trying to be reasonable at the point of crisis. If we attempt to argue, threaten, to point out the consequences or appeal to higher motives, all we are likely to do is to 'provoke' another angry and uncontrolled reaction.

In working with pupils who have become very angry, our first task is to attempt to calm them down and reduce their levels of arousal. There is some evidence that calming gestures with the palm of the hand held at about chest height, with fingers pointing upward and making gradually slower and slower up and down movements, as though patting the air, can be effective in calming people down. The open palm is a peaceful and non-aggressive gesture and the gradually slowing down of the hand movements mirrors the reduction of arousal that you are trying to achieve. Any body language, tone of voice, or body posture which displays power or dominance is likely to be much less effective in calming the person down once the initial crisis or explosive phase has passed. What we are trying to communicate in this first phase is our concern, and that we are listening.

This concern is expressed by demonstrating a level of arousal which is slightly lower than that of the angry young person. This is the strategy of 'mood matching'. If we show total calmness and are completely laid back in the face of an agitated pupil this is very likely to be interpreted as rejection or non-concern. We should try to express, by our tone of voice, speed of speech, our own body movements, that we really are concerned – but to do this in such a way that we use our own levels of arousal to gradually lower the arousal levels of the other person. Too much 'agitation' on our part is likely to 'hype' up the youngster again – too little, is likely to suggest that you are not really hearing the message. This will be met with a further escalation to make sure that you do!

Angry outbursts happen when pupils feel that they have been threatened or attacked in some way. This attack is often about being made to look small, devalued or being treated unjustly. Angry feelings are frequently due to failure in communication – either because the other person really has treated the pupil very badly or because the pupil has not been able to communicate in any other way apart from exploding into verbal or physical violence. In working with a pupil who has exploded with anger, the task of the adult is to open up communication. This is best done by listening very carefully and showing that you really are listening. This ensures that we give the message that we value the pupil. Together with the calming tactics outlined above, our first task is to give the

Figure 7.2 *The calm after the storm*

angry person feedback that we recognise that they are indeed very angry. The active listening skills of reflecting back both the meaning and the sense of what the angry pupil is saying to us is the critical first step. This is all the more important if the child's anger has been a response to something *we* have done, either by being the 'trigger' (perhaps by demanding some behaviour, or restricting the pupil in some way), or because we have been seen to 'fail' to protect the child against a threat from a third party. '*I can see you are very angry and upset because . . .*' is the message we need to get across and with it the underlying message that we distinguish between strong feelings, which are always 'legitimate' and behaviours which may not be.

When arousal levels have been reduced to a level such that 'rationality' has a chance (and we need to remember that this probably involves a longer time than we may realise), then we have two further tasks to achieve. The first is to help solve the problem that has caused the perceived threat to the child's self esteem and the second is re-establish the real world with consequences for any unacceptable behaviour.

As regards the first, we have to try to achieve a very delicate balance between calming the child down on the one hand and solving the problem on the other. Carry on with the calming too long and we risk another outburst because we are seen as doing nothing about the problem (which is usually to do with a perceived injustice or attack); step in too soon with solutions to the problem, before the child is calm enough to engage in problem solving, and we can find ourselves with more thunder and lightning!

The problem solving phase begins with trying to establish the facts about the incident which has triggered the emotional reaction. Here it is important to convey that we are not attempting to judge the truth of the account or the justification for the child feeling aggrieved. Our role is very much that of a non-judgemental counsellor, using all the skills of open and closed questioning, paraphrasing and summarising what is being said to us, and reflecting back the emotions and feelings that we are picking up from verbal and non-verbal communication. This active listening stage is followed by what may need to be done to close the incident and start afresh.

This will usually involve repairing the sense of injustice that the child has experienced. As an adult, this may mean protecting the pupil from further provocation, minimising the presence of the trigger as far as possible. In some cases it may mean the adult acting to restore a sense of fairness and to stop the behaviour of the person which was the trigger of the outburst. In other situations it may be more a matter of exploring with the youngster different ways of handling future situations, using some of the techniques which derive from behavioural, psychodynamic and cognitive approaches. Such interventions may clearly need much more time than is available in the space following the outburst. Instead, a message conveying that we would like to explore these issues in more depth at a later date would need to be given – and in a way which is seen by the pupil as being supportive and helpful.

The second aspect which needs to be addressed requires very careful handling and it relates once again to the important distinction we have consistently emphasised, namely that between the felt emotion and the behaviour. In a violent outburst, the behaviour almost by definition is likely to be destructive and damaging, either to the self, or to other people (adults or children), or to property. It is very important that the pupil perceives that there are consequences which will follow from the unacceptable behaviour. The pupil needs to be alerted to this fact in a quiet and unemotional way, and it is probably very good advice to leave it there at this point. The detailed connection between behaviour and the precise consequences needs to be left to much later in the process, preferably several hours after the end of the outburst and even till the following day. It is likely that if the issue is handled sensitively then, when normal levels of physiological arousal have returned, that the pupil will be able to see the consequences of overstepping clearly defined boundaries as acceptable and just.

Experience suggests that if adults, and particularly those in higher authority, step in too soon, when physiological levels have not returned to normal and start to lay down the law, often with emotion themselves, and start to administer punishment for unacceptable behaviour, a further eruption is likely to take place, simply compounding the issue further. It is better to wait until all emotions have cooled off and then unemotionally to put in place consequences that have previously been clearly established. The importance of whole-school policies and clear hierarchies of both rewards and consequences enable this process to avoid many of the side effects of 'punishment', which when handled badly simply increase the perceived devaluing of the pupil, rather than the unacceptability of the behaviour. A closed chapter and a fresh start is more likely if the pupil does not feel 'punished'.

In the longer term, when the storm has clearly passed by and sunshine, and perhaps, showers have returned, there is work still to be done, but this will be preventative and no longer at crisis levels. We will certainly need to help the pupil learn how to avoid further explosions and to keep their fireworks safe. This work is frequently to do with developing communication skills so that the pupil has alternative ways of expressing and coping with strong emotions in more socially acceptable ways.

Earlier in the book, and in this chapter, we have discussed ideas about preventing or managing problem anger. In the next chapter we will consider specific ways of helping individual children to manage their anger more effectively.

Summary

- Intense anger is accompanied by high levels of physiological arousal.

- There is no point in trying to reason with an extremely angry person – wait until they have really calmed down: this may take much longer than you think!

- The first task is to listen. Acknowledge that you see the pupil is very angry about something.

- The second task is to help the pupil solve the problem that triggered the outburst

- Distinguish between behaviours which may be unacceptable and the emotions which are legitimate.

Action

Practise the active listening skills which are crucially important in working with a pupil who has become very angry. How do *you* convey to someone that you are really listening (body posture, tone of voice, eye contact)? Practice the skill of reflective listening and paraphrasing.

In the problem solving phrase, remember the four steps:

1. Start with getting the pupil to tell you in clear factual language what happened.

2. Help the pupil to think up alternatives for handling the situation and to choose one.

3. Make sure they have the skills to carry it out.

4. Give them the opportunity to talk to you again about how they have got on.

THE FIREWORKS

Chapter 8

Working with angry children

Troubled and troubling children, who often get angry, are able to be helped in a variety of ways. Such help is at its most effective when directed at helping children to help themselves, so that they can regain the power to have their needs appropriately met. William Glasser (1986) suggests that humans have *five basic needs*:

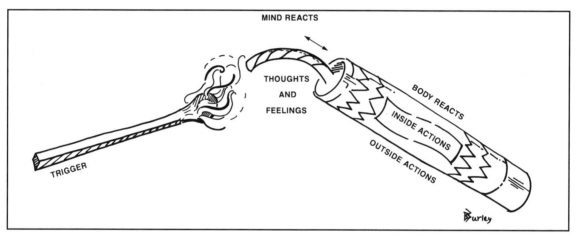

Figure 8.1 *The Firework Model*

Figure 8.2 *The Firework Model made real: a common trigger*

- to survive and reproduce

- to belong and love

- to gain power

- to be free

- to have fun

Children who have little or no anger control are less likely to meet these needs without violating the best interests of others.

Beyond the needs outlined above are 'higher level' needs as described by Abraham Maslow (1968). Specifically, he includes *ego needs* which encompass self-respect, self-confidence, achievement, and competence. At the top of Maslow's pyramid there is *self-actualisation* which occurs when a person realises his or her full potential, a relatively rare phenomenon. For very angry children the reality is that Maslow's 'lower level' needs are the likely focus for any support work offered by responsible adults, including parents, carers, teachers, and other professionals. These needs include:

- *Physical* – air, food, rest, shelter

- *Safety* – protection against danger, threat, deprivation, freedom from fear

- *Social* – belonging, association, acceptance, giving and receiving love and friendship

Sadly, there are a significant number of children who are so troubled that immediate support and direction may be necessary to ensure their safety or the safety of others, and such intrusive management of behaviour is described in the next chapter in the context of crisis management. Reactive strategies designed to manage dangerous behaviour are only acceptable as a short-term expedient and should be a prelude to moving children on to becoming more receptive to understanding and helping themselves.

An activity that helps children of varying age and ability to begin to develop an understanding of their anger is the use of a behaviour diary or anger log (preferably produced by the child herself, or with minimum help). This log (see Appendix 2) can then be used to complete an Anger thermometer (Figure 8.3). The use of these tools allows a child to identify their 'triggers', and then in discussion with a responsible adult, to describe suitable options for managing such people, events, things, or places in the future.

Such an approach can be used at home to help deal more effectively with problem areas including feeding, toileting, hygiene, sibling rivalry, homework, tidiness. Younger children will need more help to identify options, and parents and carers will need

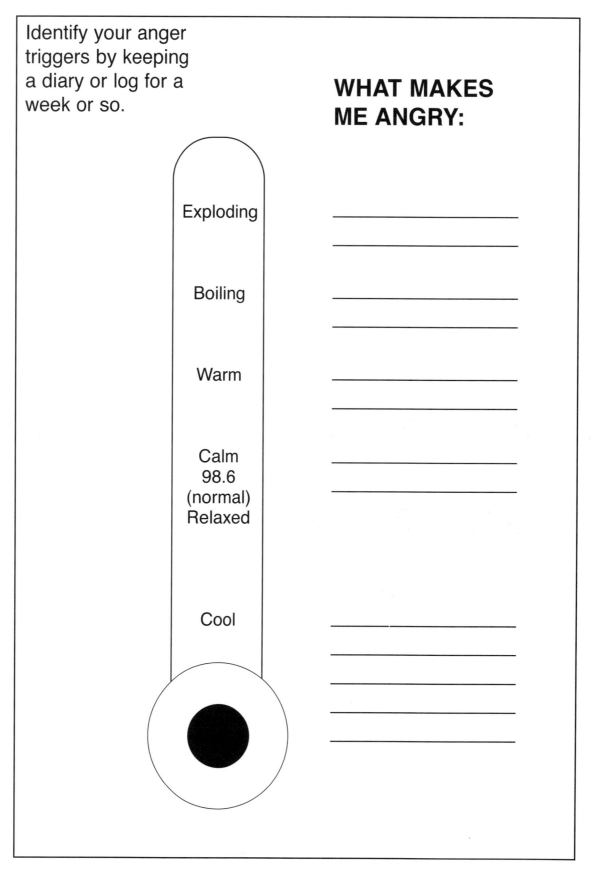

Figure 8.3 Anger thermometer

Figure 8.4 *The firework explodes*

to reward good choices more immediately and frequently.

In the school setting this approach could be used to identify targets for inclusion in Individual Education Plans (IEPs), and would be particularly valuable for helping the child or young person to become more involved in devising a plan designed to improve their anger management.

Following discussion in Chapter 2 about the importance of our own thoughts, feelings, and actions, it is important to note that the behaviour log and anger thermometer might also be usefully completed by parents, carers, teachers and others at the same time as the child identified as having difficulty managing anger. This exercise could potentially have two benefits; firstly reframing the problem and so move key people on from viewing the difficulty as exclusively 'within child', and secondly letting the child feel that adults are continually having to work hard to manage their anger too.

In addition to the above, a range of 'crafty tactics', skills, and techniques can be used in work with angry children to avoid the inevitable explosion (Figure 8.4). These are:

1. distraction

2. relocation

3. do something different

4. use humour

5. active listening

6. active ignoring

7. self-talk and self-calming techniques

8. behaviour modification (including assertive discipline and assertive parenting)

9. conflict resolution

10. teaching good behaviour

11. peer mediation

12. therapeutic metaphor (stories that heal)

13. social skills training

14. anger spoilers (for example count to 10, or 100!)

The *defusing* techniques (numbers 1 to 5) are usefully employed by teachers and carers with children and young people of all ages, though clearly they need to be implemented in an age-appropriate way. Defusing techniques were more fully described in Chapter 6.

The *skill-building* techniques (numbers 6 to 14) need to be taught to children and young people, with subsequent reinforcement and monitoring. Additionally some of these techniques are complex and sophisticated and may be well beyond the current repertoire of many teachers and carers, thereby necessitating support or training from other professionals such as educational psychologists. Each of these eight techniques are described below.

Active ignoring This technique involves consciously choosing to ignore troubling or challenging behaviour for the sake of expediency and longer-term gain. For example, if a child uses bad language but under his breath, a teacher may be wise to let it go and focus on getting the child to do something positive. Many confrontations are actually provoked by teachers and carers worrying away at every minor behavioural or rule infringement.

Self-talk and self-calming techniques These techniques need to be taught at a time when the child or young person is calm and behaving fairly rationally. In addition the child must recognise that their anger can be problematic, and ideally be interested in learning to handle it more effectively. To reach this point may require a number of sessions examining how their angry outbursts cost them dearly (see the Anger Pie, Chapter 3, Figure 3.1), possibly keeping a diary or behaviour log and using an Anger thermometer to identify the times when they are likely to 'blow'.

Self-talk involves a child recognising the early warning signs before rage develops and then using 'cool-it' thoughts, words and actions. For example, if a child knows that insults directed at her mother have led to massive anger in the past, then teach her a buzz-word to trigger positive thinking, such as 'supercool'. This can then be used to trigger some 'taught' thoughts, such as: '*I can hack this . . . I've been here before and I can get past this positively.*' If the provocation increases then repetition is needed and other strategies need to have been taught too. Self-talk is likely to work best only at the earliest stages of anger, and is not an end in itself.

Combining self-talk with breathing and relaxation techniques is likely to be even more effective, so deep breathing in through the nose and gently out through the mouth can be coupled with 'I can hack this, I will hack this'.

Self-calming may be further enhanced by actions coupled with self-talk, such as finger counting using the thumb of the right hand against the fingers, preferably discretely so as not to draw attention to it. Alternatively simply place a hand near the diaphragm so the breathing can be easily monitored.

Children who frequently display problem anger will need very structured teaching and opportunities for overlearning of these techniques if they are to become embedded in their intuitive repertoire of behaviours. Additionally, some authors argue that it's important not to let the self-calming techniques become obsessional and problematic behaviour themselves.

Behaviour modification (including assertive discipline and assertive parenting)

Assertive discipline is a systematic and structured programme designed to help teachers and carers help children to learn by giving clear, reasonable, and consistent messages about what a child has to do, then routinely rewarding them for successful behaviour or implementing negative consequences for failing to follow these messages. Training in an assertive discipline programme typically takes about a day, but the following features of the programme give a flavour of the content:

- Assertive communication.

- Say what you mean, mean what you say, and ideally say it once (but be prepared to repeat it if necessary).

- Use clear unambiguous messages framed positively, e.g. 'I want you to get your book out now' (then praise).

- Catch children being good (instead of responding to their bad behaviour).

- Use positive non-verbal communication to back up, reinforce, or instead of, verbal communication, e.g. head shake for 'no' and nodding for 'yes'.

- Use the 'broken record technique', namely repeat your request calmly up to three times (if there is still no compliance be prepared to take preplanned action).

Back your communication with action
- If a child does not comply after repeated requests, issue a warning.

- If non-compliance continues, impose a negative consequence, e.g. staying behind for one minute after class, further non-compliance results in two minutes after class.

Consequences should only be imposed according to a published plan, and never arbitrarily or unexpectedly. Here are two commonly used plans found to be helpful.

Teachers plan	*Carers plan*
Warning	Warning
1 minute after class	5 minutes early to bed
2 minutes after class	10 minutes early to bed
Send to senior teacher	Miss a favourite TV programme
Parents called	Grounded for a weekend

Consequences must never violate the best interests of the child, and should be provided as close to the time of the behaviour as possible.

Other forms of behaviour modification might include the use of a chart with stickers or stars with written targets, preferably agreed with the child. At school these would typically be about conforming to expected behaviour standards, whilst at home they might be about getting equipment together for school or coming in at an agreed time. Again, praise and positive reinforcement are the keys to success, so reward successive approximations to the desired goals and keep the targets WARM (*W*orkable, *A*chievable, *R*ealistic, and *M*anageable).

Conflict resolution

At school, conflict resolution is probably best taught as part of a Personal, Social, and Health Education (PSHE) curriculum. If taught to everybody, rather than just children with excessive problem anger, it is likely to be more effective and underpinned by explicit value statements such as:

'Respect each person's right to have their own point of view'
'Always try to understand *how* other people feel'
'Get your needs met without violating (hurting) the best interests of others'

Deriving a set of value statements that children and young people can own is best undertaken by involving them. Many schools continue to struggle with over-ambitious imposed values, which are ineffective because they are not owned by the pupils.

At home, conflict resolution is likely to be a far more volatile process than at school, since parents and most carers are not paid professionals with a job description and external appraisal!

For parents and teachers alike, trying to teach children appropriate and useful conflict resolution skills is underpinned by one simple rule:

Aim for a Win/Win solution!

Consider this simple 'outcome matrix' for resolving conflict between one adult (parent or teacher) and one child, e.g. *Getting homework done on time*:

Child	Adult
Win	Win
Lose	Win
Win	Lose
Lose	Lose

Accept that 'everybody wins' equally is an unlikely outcome if the issue is at all contentious, but nevertheless try to give both parties something to feel good about. Acknowledge too that this dynamic becomes increasingly complex as the group size increases, e.g. in a class with one teacher and 30 children. However, the following are simple guidelines to promote positive conflict resolution.

- Do not try to resolve conflict if someone is still angry (wait for up to 45 minutes after an outburst).

- Teach alternatives to displaying problem anger (see 'Anger spoilers' below).

- Only use 'I messages', for example, for a teacher: 'I feel frustrated when people wander around the classroom'; for a pupil: 'I often worry about my homework'.

- Try to adopt a 'no blame' culture – for a teacher do *not* say: 'I feel frustrated when you wander around the classroom'; for a pupil, do *not* say: 'I often worry about my homework when *you* tell me to get it done'.

- Try the 'Step into my shoes' or 'See it through my eyes' routine, where each person has to explain the problem as the other person sees it.

- Acknowledge your part of the problem, however small that is – for example, 'I can see that it could be irritating to be told to do something you don't like doing'.

- Identify solutions or part-solutions as a shared activity, then choose one that is as close to win/win as you can.

- Be generous next time if your win is bigger this time!

Teaching good behaviour

In order to help children learn to read, most schools have curriculum leaders, schemes of work, lesson plans, monitoring, benchmarking, training for teachers, resources, and home–school links. However, astonishingly few schools have an explicit programme for teaching good behaviour, which is even more curious since many of them report that concerns about behaviour are at, or near to, the top of their agenda.

Working on the premise that actions speak louder than words, Teaching Good Behaviour is best begun by helping children to do good things, whether they want to or not. Very angry children need help to see themselves as 'good', since they have had considerable experience of feeling the reverse. There are at least two benefits resulting from angry children doing good things: firstly, they develop a sense of themselves as 'good', thereby boosting self-esteem; and secondly, their image is improved in the eyes of others (peers, parents, teachers etc.).

Lawrence Shapiro and others (1994) describe how the publishing company, Conari Press produced a series of stories called *Random Acts of Kindness* which ultimately started a national movement in the USA, whereby children in classrooms across the country try to do one kind thing a day. Examples of 'kind actions' include: opening a door for someone else; saying something encouraging to someone who is sad; putting some small change into a charity collection. The kindness may be contagious, but even if not, each act is a positive behaviour.

Teachers and parents can help in the teaching of good behaviour by:

- ensuring that children are noticed doing at least one good thing each day;

- encouraging children to keep their own log of good deeds and perhaps have a cumulative reward;

- give clear and simple directions on how to behave positively;

- link to behaviour modification programmes, such as the use of star charts.

Peer mediation   Peer mediation involves fellow pupils or students acting as a mediator, which means being a neutral third party who tries to resolve conflict or dispute between two or more other children. Mediators need to understand the principles of conflict resolution, which involves training, and then be closely supervised by a skilled adult.

Guidelines for a mediator would include:

- be a good listener;

- show you have heard and understood by 'telling back' to the person speaking;

- give everyone an equal chance to give their story or view;

- stay on the fence . . . whatever you think don't take sides;

- as soon as the dispute or conflict is identified, get the children in conflict to come up with solutions or ideas of how to move forward.

And the stages of mediation are:

(a) Set the *ground rules*
- allow each person to talk and listen without interruption
- enter the mediation expecting to solve the problem
- agree to be bound by the agreed rules and the solution generated.

(b) *Define the problem* or dispute (with each child).

(c) *Identify solutions* without discussion of their merits.

(d) *Choose a solution* that everyone can live with.

(e) See if there is a way of avoiding *similar conflict* in the future.

(f) *Finish positively* – 'Well done everyone for sorting this out'.

Therapeutic metaphor (stories that heal)

Storytelling or therapeutic metaphors essentially involve projecting a problem onto someone or something else (other people, places or objects) as way of successfully dealing with strong emotions in a safe and relatively unthreatening way. If a 'dangerous' story is retold in a more solution-focused way, using metaphor, then many children with problem anger can be more open to the indirect messages than simply being told how better to respond or behave.

Richard Gardner (in Shapiro 1994) has developed the Mutual Storytelling Technique over the last 25 years and suggests that children with Conduct Disorders (challenging or acting-out behaviour often characterised by considerable problem anger) are deficient in their sense of guilt about their behaviour. Storytelling can enable the child to reframe guilt into a more positive emotion, by developing, instead a sense of remorse, whilst at the same time exploring how the child might use this sense of remorse to avoid problem anger in the future. Effectively this is equivalent to promoting super-ego controls in psychoanalytic terms, or creating more appropriate self-talk in cognitive terms.

The Mutual Storytelling Technique involves a child in choosing an object and then telling a story about it. For example, Gardner describes children picking from a bag of toys which contains animals, people, common objects, monsters, and so on. The child then tells a story about the toy and draws a lesson or moral from the story. The therapist can then pick a toy and tell a positive or corrective story, using a similar theme, but having the main character act in a way which involves making good prosocial choices and displaying personal responsibility. This technique can be further enhanced by linking it to behaviour modification, whereby the child for example gets points or tokens for choosing a toy and more points for telling a story, and points can be accumulated and used for suitable rewards. If this technique is used over time, then the child's work can be built into a personal book or anthology of stories, and these can be illustrated either by the child or using montage, clip-art, or photographs. A common underlying theme can often be highlighted, which aims to empower the child to deal more effectively with their problem anger in real life.

In practice, such work goes on in schools under the heading of 'creative writing' where it is a feature of either the English or PSHE curricula. However, engaging in this work in a therapeutic context requires training and supervision. Such training for teachers, often called 'educational therapy' has been available for over 25 years, but only from a limited number of institutions in Britain such as the Tavistock Clinic in London.

Social skills training

A differentiated social skills curriculum needs to be devised by each school, which is endorsed and supported by parents and carers and underpinned by a minimum set of core values. The aim of such a curriculum is to foster the development of all children and young people by teaching them to behave in a prosocial way. Typically, schools build this into their PSHE curriculum to a greater or lesser extent, but it may be argued that many children need a far more structured and competency-based teaching model than is generally found in Britain. Specific components of an effective curriculum might include the following:

- ability to *introduce yourself and others* in a group setting

- good *listening* skills

- make appropriate *eye contact* and good use of other *non-verbal skills*

- good *turn-taking* skills

- ability to *share* appropriately

- good *speaking* skills; rate, tone, volume

- ability to follow reasonable *directions*

- ability to follow *rules* of play, games, classroom

- *join in groups* for tasks and fun

- *ignore provocation* and other distractions

- *express views, feelings, ideas* appropriately

- *seek help* appropriately

- *receive praise*

- *manage anger* (own and others)

- form and maintain *successful relationships* with peers and adults

This list is not exhaustive, though many other skills can be subsumed within the various components. Each of the skills are open to creative teaching methods such as drama, role play, journalism, community service, games, outward-bound activities, and sport. Sadly, curriculum pressures and competing demands for time often result in less creative approaches being used in many schools, with the result that students frequently reject PSHE as unimportant or low priority. Paradoxically, teachers complain of spending increasing amounts of time in 'managing behaviour' at the same time as spending less time teaching students how to behave.

Anger spoilers

These are simply 'mini-strategies' for children, and adults, to use to prevent anger building up or getting out of control. Some of these are related to some of the defusing techniques and all are capable of immediate implementation at the point when an individual feels the mental or physical charging-up of anger. These are to be used either when the 'trigger' has been spotted or 'the fuse is lit', but *before* any 'explosion':

- *count to 10* (or if need be 100!) before taking action

- *punch a pillow or bobo doll* (allegedly cathartic, and some schools of management even use this technique with executives!)

- *take exercise* – activities involving movement

- *tell someone* in charge (which needs to be taken seriously by teachers or carers)

- use the *stuck CD* or *broken record technique* (e.g. keep telling the person provoking you 'I feel hurt when you call me names but I'm going to ignore it')

- use the *turtle technique*, pretending to be protected by a shell and simply not responding to any provocation

- walk away

- be *disarming or charming* (e.g. 'I'm sorry you feel the need to say hurtful things, because I actually like you/want to like you')

Even in a school, or at home, where most of these strategies are being used there will still be occasional crises. The focus of the next chapter is planning, in advance, how to stay in charge and deal with crises caused by problem anger.

Summary

We all need

- to survive and reproduce

- to belong and love

- to gain power

- to be free

- to have fun

There are available a range of tactics, skills and techniques to help children manage their anger:

1. distraction

2. relocation

3. do something different

4. use humour

5. active ignoring

6. active listening

7. self-talk and self-calming techniques

8. behaviour modification (including assertive discipline and assertive parenting)

9. conflict resolution

10. teaching good behaviour

11. peer mediation

12. therapeutic metaphor (stories that heal)

13. social skills training

14. anger spoilers

Action

For a child who is experiencing excessive problem anger get them to:

1. Keep a diary or behaviour log for one week (including good and angry behaviour).

2. Ask parent(s) and teacher(s) to contribute to the diary/log.

3. Identify three positive target behaviours for the child to work on for the following week.

4. Select at least three of the tactics or skills listed as numbers 7 to 14 above (see 'Summary'), and teach the child how they might use them to meet their targets.

5. Select and use three of the tactics from the defusing strategies numbered 1 to 6 above (see 'Summmary'). Both teacher and parents can use these tactics.

6. Closely monitor, support and encourage the child for the next two weeks, celebrating movement towards the desired targets.

7. After two weeks review the targets and modify them or identify new ones and continue as above.

Chapter 9

Crisis management

Introduction   In earlier chapters we have discussed the possibility of defusing problem anger at the point at which the early warning signs of an angry outburst are identified. We have also identified ways of trying to avoid the storm, either through environmental means (e.g. whole-school approaches), or through diffusing individual anger (e.g. by using calming techniques. The importance of teaching children and young people alternative ways of viewing the behaviours of other people, and more effective ways to communicate strong feelings, has also been discussed. There will be times, however, when all the appropriate measures are in place to reduce the probability of an angry outburst, but we still have to respond when children have lost control and are a danger to themselves or others. This is when individuals are in the crisis stage of the Assault Cycle, and are so physiologically aroused, that they are unable to be rational and unable to see someone else's point of view. At this point we need to know how to minimise the effects of a young person's 'explosion'.

We will begin with practical responses at the point of crisis; go on to discuss how school policy can support these responses; discuss physical intervention as a last resort when all other options have been attempted and there is a real danger to safety, and finally look at the importance of debriefing after being involved in a violent incident.

Practical   The following guidance relates to the responses adapted at the time
responses   the crisis erupts.

Do

- remain controlled – keeping completely calm is both unlikely and may be unhelpful as discussed in earlier chapters with reference to mood matching, but maintaining controlled responses is very important; a high degree of rationality and a low degree of emotionality should be aimed for;

- talk firmly and with clear directions, e.g. 'Stop that now', 'Put that down'; you may have to use the broken record technique (see Chapter 7) to reinforce your directions;

- keep talking;

- locate, and move towards, the exits;

- call for help;

- tell the pupil you are calling for help in order to support them and help them regain control;

- remove any audience;

- remove other people if they are in danger;

- remove potential weapons;

- keep a safe distance – violent people tend to need more body space than others;

- assume that the person is going to calm quickly;

- in the case of fights between two pupils, remove the audience and encourage the least aggressive to move away and seek more help if necessary; loud noises, e.g. a whistle, can be effective in distracting pupils out of their aggression temporarily.

Don't

- use confrontational body language – side to side is less confrontational than face to face;

- engage in prolonged or exaggerated eye contact;

- use confrontational or provocative language, e.g. 'Stop being so childish', 'Act your age';

- use physical intervention unless other non-physical methods of calming have been tried, and there are significant risks to personal safety.

School policy

There should be a policy which specifies a clear action plan for staff who find themselves having to deal with pupils who have lost control. This should incorporate the need for consistency across the school. Staff who are prepared and know what they are going to do in the event of a crisis will feel confident that they have a planned response, rather than anxious and unsure. Pupils who have emotional difficulties respond well to adults who display a confident air of being in control. Most young people need to feel that they can be controlled by others and find their own lack of control very frightening. The more confident the adult is the more quickly a young person is likely to calm.

The policy should include:

- a mechanism for obtaining support from another member of staff;

- guidance on who stays with the class and who stays with the pupil in distress: a fresh member of staff who has not been involved in the conflict may be more likely to calm the pupil, but if the class teacher has a particularly good relationship with that pupil, it may be better for them to do the calming;

- a requirement for individual education plans (as identified by the Code of Practice, see DfE 1994), for those pupils showing frequent outbursts, to cover the teaching of appropriate ways of dealing with anger, appropriate calming techniques and directions on how to handle violent outbursts.

- how to record the incident effectively;

- when and how to involve parents;

- when and how to involve other agencies;

- guidelines on physical intervention that are in line with LEA policy;

- when and how to debrief from the incident – to allow those involved to resolve strong feelings that have been engendered, to allow calming from physiological arousal and to rebuild relationships with the pupil;

- when and how to discuss what can be done to reduce the probability of the incident happening again.

It is important that all staff are involved in developing an appropriate policy for their particular circumstances and that there are opportunities to practise the procedures involved in order to increase confidence. The importance of developing strategies to avoid violent outbursts cannot be over emphasised.

Physical intervention

The term physical intervention has been used to replace physical restraint as there have been negative connotations attached to the term restraint in the past. Physical intervention should only be used as a last resort and should not be considered unless all other methods of calming have been found to be unhelpful for the pupil.

If it is considered to be a necessary strategy, then clear policy guidelines should be followed and ideally staff should be trained and confident in using approved methods. Physical intervention:

- must only be used in an emergency; where a real danger to personal safety is perceived, either to yourself, the pupil, or other persons'; or where there is risk of causing significant damage to property;

- must be in the pupil's best interests – not simply to get the pupil to do what you want him or her to;

- must be the minimum necessary to prevent harm;

- must not be used as an aversive consequence or punishment;

- must assist the pupil to regain control;

- must not cause the pupil harm;

- must only be used until the pupil has calmed;

- must not be a substitute for positive behaviour management strategies;

- must be recorded in writing;

- must be discussed with parents.

Physical intervention with pupils always carries an element of physical risk and as such should not be entered into unless the perceived risks of not intervening are greater. The legal implications of physical interventions should be considered at a whole-school level. Useful guidance to the law is found in *Legal Issues* (Lyon 1994).

When any intervention plan is being devised, a risk analysis should be considered to support the rationale for intervening, or not doing so, in particular circumstances. In this way the balance between adult control and individual rights can be effectively considered. (A useful guide providing more detail is '*Physical Interventions: A Policy Framework*' (Harris *et al.* 1997).)

The foregoing relates to pupils who are having difficulty controlling their anger and are losing control when anger is triggered by an event or perceived threat. It does not relate to self-defence issues, where a person is deliberately trying to attack someone. This is not within the scope of this book.

Debriefing

Debriefing is often overlooked but it is vital to the development of strategies to stabilise or improve the emotional health of those involved in violent outbursts.

Maintaining emotional health necessitates short-term and long-term strategies for all of us. Short-term strategies should include opportunities to recover from the trauma of violent outbursts. It is likely that the crisis has left all those involved feeling emotionally and physically drained. Opportunities to calm physically should exist with opportunities, both for the adult and the pupil, to discuss the crisis. To develop long-term strategies will be necessary to understand the events that led up to the outburst; think about ways of avoiding similar outbursts in the future, consider whether responses were effective, and depersonalise issues that are outside of our control. Ways of rebuilding relationships with the pupil will need to be considered, and residual feelings, for example anger or guilt, of both the adult and the pupil will need to be resolved.

Conclusion
This chapter has looked at ways of dealing with crises when a young person displays problem anger to the point of losing control. This is the Crisis stage of the Assault Cycle. Pupils who have lost control through the use of stimulants or because of psychiatric difficulties have not been discussed in this chapter. This is not to say that the general principles of calming and planning are not appropriate, but that other strategies may need to be employed as well. Particular advice from experts in these fields should be sought in these instances.

In the final chapter we are writing directly for parents and carers. Most of the advice holds good for teachers and other professionals too.

Summary

To minimise the effects of a young person's angry outburst, it is necessary to consider the following:

- practical responses – Dos and Don'ts

- whole-school policy

- physical intervention

- debriefing

Action

- Check your school policy to ensure it includes clear guidelines for managing violent incidents.

- Find out if your LEA has guidelines on physical intervention – familiarise yourself with them, or develop some.

- Practise relaxation techniques to encourage your own emotional and physical health.

Chapter 10

Help for parents and carers

Understanding and managing anger in children

There is anger in every child and in every family – that much is certain! What is not so clear is

- *why* some children show much more anger than others

- at what point levels of anger become *worrisome*

- how best to *respond* to anger when it arises

Some child psychologists, Melanie Klein for example (see Segal 1992), see anger as an inevitable part of normal development. Whether those feelings of hate and anger in the infant and toddler persist, depends very much on how certain basic needs of the young child are met.

Our model of anger sees it as primarily a negative emotion, connected biologically to a perceived threat. The response of anger is one of 'fight' rather than 'flight'. If that is true, then it becomes clear that there are numerous aspects of infancy, toddlerhood, childhood and adolescence in which the youngster is likely to perceive that they are being 'attacked'. Remember, the important thing is that the person *perceives* themselves as being 'attacked' – it is almost irrelevant as to whether this corresponds in any way with what is really happening. It is also worth pointing out that a world which does not immediately comply with the child's strongly felt desires can be seen as needing to be fought against desperately, and sometimes viciously. The 'world', that is you the parents, or brothers and sisters, 'should' not, 'must' not, thwart me from getting the things I see as 'mine'. It simply must not give me anything I don't want either. So, there are going to be innumerable occasions throughout our early years when issues of 'control' and 'power' are potentially occasions for frustration, which may then spill over into anger, either with or without feelings of being persecuted and singled out for attack.

We have seen also that when we feel we are being attacked, psychologically or physically, some of us do not fight, but run away. There are a number of reasons as to why some children respond to perceived threat with anxiety (running away), and others with anger (standing up and fighting back). Which way of acting becomes dominant largely seems to depend upon which strategy is modelled to us by our parents or which one seems to bring us the most immediate feelings of security. Of course, neither anger nor anxiety is likely to be a really effective strategy in the long run, as neither of them help us to feel valued and secure in the longer term. A very general principle – easy to say, but notoriously difficult to work out in day to day living, is that the most effective way to prevent the development of angry children and adolescents is to convey to them a sense of worth and unique value. It seems that all our perceived threats really come down to being seen as attacks upon this sense of value. The most effective antidote to anger (or anxiety) is a genuine, passively received message that 'I am valued and loveable'. The more we genuinely feel valued, the less likely that we will feel angry, with its accompanying tactics of spite, hurt, put downs, hate, envy and jealousy.

Children and young people get angry about different things at different stages as they grow up. Some of course do not develop emotionally as they should and continue to act in ways that we accept in young childhood, but which are completely unacceptable in adolescence. We expect a two or three year old to be experiencing total rage and frustration and not having strategies to cope with this, so that we may have to physically take control until the tantrum subsides: we consider it very worrying if a fourteen or fifteen year old, frustrated in his or her desires for 'freedom', launches into the same intensity of being out of control. We expect the door slam, the sulks and moodiness, the muttering. This may be infuriating, but quite normal.

Differences in anger as children grow up

So one dimension as we move from infancy through childhood into adolescence is the degree of 'self control' which we can expect. The younger the child, the more raw and uninhibited is the emotion felt and expressed. We do not really know what very young infants 'feel', except through their very obvious behaviour – mothers 'read' how their babies are feeling by what they see in terms of activity level, body tone, type of cry, and most of all, facial expressions. The importance of these non-verbal signals that we give to others about our 'true' feelings remains throughout life, but of course we quickly develop the extraordinarily sophisticated tool of language to communicate our inner state to others and to ourselves. As the infant develops into a toddler, the rawness and immediacy of emotional reaction to others and being thwarted begins to give way to signs of self regulation. By the age of two, for example, we see attempts to 'control' negative emotions, by, for example, wrinkled brows and lip biting. This is not something that simply happens with the mere passage of time (simple maturation) but something we learn from others around us. We learn to inhibit our emotional expression, to channel these emotions in socially acceptable ways and to develop strategies for dealing with strong emotions. Children as young as three can in some circumstances deliberately hide their true feelings and this skill develops as the child grows older. We are increasingly able to put on a brave face or go quiet when upset and angry.

What do children get angry about?

Although there can be innumerable types of things that children become angry about, there do seem to be issues which are characteristic of certain ages. Temper tantrums of two to three year olds and the moodiness and tetchyness of adolescence are examples.

Erik Erikson (1950) thought that we go through eight distinct stages as we grow up and that in each stage we have particular tasks to achieve. If we do not master the task of a particular stage it makes it much harder for us to tackle the next one. Each stage brings with it its own tensions and frustrations, particular issues about which we are very vulnerable and unduly sensitive – and it is these issues which can be perceived as being a threat to us and thus sparking off intense anger.

Stages of childhood

The earliest stage, that of infancy, is where the basic task is that of achieving a basic trust in the world and in people. This is something that we acquire with the sense of 'bonding' with loving and caring mother/father figures. The overall balance of our major needs for food, warmth, affection and care being met is such that we come to see the world as basically trustworthy. The failure to achieve this results in a 'basic mistrust', where we see the world as persecutory and threatening and thus we become suspicious, quick to perceive attack and hurt. Children who have suffered emotional and physical neglect and abuse carry with them a suspiciousness and hostility which is very hard to shift.

The second stage, roughly that of the toddler, is characterised by physically standing on one's own two feet, in walking and being able to do a whole variety of new skills. The issue centres around 'autonomy', a sense of being upright and holding one's head up high. Battles over physical control become dominant, often showing themselves in screams and tantrums about toileting. Because toddlers are now able to do many new things but want to do even more, but do not always have the skills to do them, they become easily frustrated, kicking screaming, crying and generally flailing when they cannot be in control and have their own way. This is the stage of the classic tantrum. The ability of children to pick the worst times, the most embarrassing moments to display the 'mother-and-father' of a tantrum is the common experience of many parents. It often leads to us giving-in to stop the child continuing with the wobbler and that leaves us feeling humiliated and guilty. Often tantrums are triggered by tiredness, not feeling well, over-excitement and when parents themselves are stressed. The lack of adequate language to communicate to you their needs simply adds to the likelihood of the child losing control in a mixture of grief and anger.

At such times you need to try to re-establish control by modelling calmness and by the use of simple, quiet words to get feelings across. The worst response is to become very angry yourself; in such a state you are unable to provide the experience of boundaries and control the child desperately needs.

The advent of a younger sibling at this age may be experienced as a loss of attention – the subtle and not so subtle pinches and pulls to a new baby are motivated by a jealousy and envy which has strangely angry overtones.

The opposite of achieving an overall sense of autonomy is that of shame and doubt, which can fester away accompanied by a sense of injustice, with the 'chip on the shoulder' variety of anger, with the person unable to rejoice in others' successes, snidely putting other people down at every opportunity. A passive anger, but anger nevertheless.

The immediate pre-school and school-entry stage is one of continuing rapid emotional, physical and intellectual growth. Erikson sees the main task to be achieved as one of establishing 'initiative'. Wanting to do everything by themselves, spurning adult help but making a 'pig's ear' of it and then becoming angry and frustrated because they have done so, it often seems as if parents simply cannot win! The temptation to step in and do things *for* our child can actually thwart that necessary drive for independence and initiative, and lead to the unadventurous and guilty child who grows into adolescent and then adult who has repressed ambitions and emotions, with the lid tightly kept shut. Such people, seemingly unemotional, can burst into furious rage when the lid begins to loosen. It is often the fear of such destructive rage that itself prevents the show of *any* emotion.

And so we come to school age. Erikson described the task here as one of establishing 'industry', and by that he meant the sense of worth that comes from achieving things by work and effort. The balance of play and work shifts – the skills to be acquired often demand hard work and effort such as learning to read, to spell, to count. For the first time, too, the family is not all important – other authority figures, such as teachers, supplement and sometimes contend with that of the parents in terms of expertise and knowledge. The schoolchild is now being compared with his or her peers, and friendships are part of that feeling of belonging. This now becomes the main task and main source of threat to the child's self-esteem. Because they are sources of threat, they are also triggers for anger. The need to belong, to achieve and to have a standing and status with one's friends become top priorities. These tasks are less easily achieved if the child does not increasingly establish the ability to control and manage their anger. The ins-and-outs of friendship, susceptibility to teasing, frustration at not being as successful as others, or as successful as one's parents would like, all these provide triggers aplenty for the school-aged child. There are likely to be feelings of insecurity, particularly of jealousy, with the accompanying moan 'It's not fair'. The 'loss' of the security and support of the family, the feeling of being not liked and left out, and of being bullied and pushed around by other bigger, cleverer and prettier children can lead to a profound sense of loneliness. The failure to achieve the sense of industry is a sense of inferiority. The need to cover up a sense of doubt about one's real worth can lead to a boastfulness and the need to put others down as the way in which anger is expressed.

Finally, as far as we are concerned here, is the stage of adolescence. There is considerable evidence that this is not necessarily the age of storm and stress that perhaps the myth of adolescence would lead us to believe. It, like any other stage, has its particular tasks, and hence its particular vulnerability. Probably because they have greater strength, quicker thinking and sophisticated control of language, adults are more frightened of what adolescents can really do to themselves and others. In one sense adolescence is a bit of a recapitulation or return to some of the earlier tasks – the partial leaving of the family at the beginning of schooling, for example, in late adolescence becomes a reality, with all the threats to security that that entails. Erikson saw the major task of adolescence as being to establish a true sense of one's own identity, to grow away from being primarily somebody's son or daughter, to being somebody in their own right, with skills, values and beliefs which are theirs and nobody else's. Not surprisingly much of the conflict, stress and perceived attacks are to do with control – about who makes the decisions, about what and when. The importance of the peer group, of peer pressure and 'unsuitable friends', and outlandish clothes and behaviour, all potentially become issues about which adolescents and parents can become very angry. At the same time, puberty brings its own fears and worries. Not infrequently, feelings of anger at their own inadequacy can be displaced onto parents, turning struggles over objectively minor issues into major outbursts.

Status and acceptance become even more important in adolescence and slights from other young people are taken very seriously, with feuds between peers provoking physical and psychological bullying. The propensity for some individuals to be scapegoats and mercilessly hounded can again be a cover up for feelings of low self-esteem and anxiety about one's own status.

We have considered what anger is, what it does, and how we may be more effective in managing it. We have described strategies for preventing and reducing problem anger, and for managing our own and other people's anger. We recognise that this is a task which is never complete. We wish you success in all your efforts to help yourself and others to manage anger more effectively.

Guidance and tips for parents living with angry children are given in Appendices 7, 8 and 9, which can be photocopied. You have read the book – now, like the person in the picture, we hope you will be managing anger more effectively.

Observation checklist – primary (5–11)

Name_____ Date of birth _____ School _____

Please circle the number which *your* observations suggest is most appropriate and add any *comments* that you think are important.

	Always	*Usually*	*Sometimes*	*Never*	*Comment*
1. Comes to school/class happily	1	2	3	4	
2. Settles in class without fuss	1	2	3	4	
3. Settles in small groups easily	1	2	3	4	
4. Follows class routines	1	2	3	4	
5. Accepts teacher's directions	1	2	3	4	
6. Accepts other pupils taking the lead	1	2	3	4	
7. Appears popular with other children	1	2	3	4	
8. Has at least one good friend	1	2	3	4	
9. Plays appropriately with other children	1	2	3	4	
10. Copes well with disappointment	1	2	3	4	
11. Appears confident	1	2	3	4	
12. Feels good about themselves	1	2	3	4	
13. Concentrates well	1	2	3	4	
14. Controls anger when provoked	1	2	3	4	
15. Has insight into own behaviour	1	2	3	4	
16. Learns from mistakes	1	2	3	4	
17. Keeps hands, feet, objects to themselves	1	2	3	4	
18. Hurts self	4	3	2	1	
19. Distracts other children	4	3	2	1	
20. Hurts other children	4	3	2	1	
Total	____	____	____	____	

Best score = 20 Worst score = 80

Completed by _____ Date _____

Observation checklist – secondary (11 –16)

Name_____ Date of birth _____ School _____

Please circle the number which *your* observations suggest is most appropriate and add any *comments* that you think are important.

	Always	*Usually*	*Sometimes*	*Never*	*Comment*
1. Comes to school/class without difficulty	1	2	3	4	
2. Settles in class easily	1	2	3	4	
3. Settles in small groups easily	1	2	3	4	
4. Follows class routines	1	2	3	4	
5. Accepts teacher's directions	1	2	3	4	
6. Accepts other students taking the lead	1	2	3	4	
7. Appears popular with other students	1	2	3	4	
8. Has at least one good friend	1	2	3	4	
9. Relates well to other students	1	2	3	4	
10. Copes well with disappointment	1	2	3	4	
11. Appears confident	1	2	3	4	
12. Feels good about themselves	1	2	3	4	
13. Concentrates well	1	2	3	4	
14. Controls anger when provoked	1	2	3	4	
15. Has insight into own behaviour	1	2	3	4	
16. Learns from mistakes	1	2	3	4	
17. Keeps hands, feet, objects to themselves	1	2	3	4	
18. Hurts self	4	3	2	1	
19. Distracts other students	4	3	2	1	
20. Hurts other students	4	3	2	1	
Total	____	____	____	____	

Best score = 20 Worst score = 80

Completed by _____ Date _____

Appendix 2

Anger log

This may be completed by (a) child (b) teacher (c) parent/carer

Name _____ **School** _____

Circle the number that best describes
Anger Management

Anger at school	Poor		Good		Excellent
Monday	1	2	3	4	5
Tuesday	1	2	3	4	5
Wednesday	1	2	3	4	5
Thursday	1	2	3	4	5
Friday	1	2	3	4	5

Anger at home					
Monday	1	2	3	4	5
Tuesday	1	2	3	4	5
Wednesday	1	2	3	4	5
Thursday	1	2	3	4	5
Friday	1	2	3	4	5
Saturday	1	2	3	4	5
Sunday	1	2	3	4	5

Anger elsewhere (trips, etc)					
Monday	1	2	3	4	5
Tuesday	1	2	3	4	5
Wednesday	1	2	3	4	5
Thursday	1	2	3	4	5
Friday	1	2	3	4	5
Saturday	1	2	3	4	5
Sunday	1	2	3	4	5

Completed by: _____ (Child/Teacher/Parent)

Appendix 3

Anger triggers

When we were discussing the Firework Model, we likened the match to the **trigger** of anger for an individual. The Assault Cycle also begins with the **trigger** stage. In order to manage our anger better, we must first identify the triggers that spark us off into an angry reaction. Triggers will be events that are perceived as threats to:

- person or property

- self-identity or self-esteem

- getting our perceived needs met

Once we have identified the triggers that make us angry, we have three possibilities:

- **avoid** the triggers

- **change** the way we **think** about the triggers

- reduce the level of arousal by using **calming** techniques

The following Worksheets provide ways of addressing these issues:

1. What makes me angry?

2. What do I think?

3. How do I feel?

4. Keeping calm.

The following Worksheets can be used with young people to help them identify their own triggers, consider alternative ways of thinking about them and identify ways of keeping themselves calm. These can be used in conjunction with the Anger Thermometer (Chapter 8) and the Anger Log (Appendix 2) as appropriate.

Worksheet 1

What makes me angry?

Stop the match being lit!

Here is a list of statements describing what makes some people angry. Tick the ones that are true for you and add some of your own that have not been listed.

- When people talk about me behind my back ....
- When I get my work wrong ....
- When other people get hurt ....
- When others won't play with me ....
- When I'm treated unfairly ....
- When I'm shouted at ....
- When people interfere with my games ....
- When people stop me doing what I want to ....
- When others get more attention than me ....
- When people call me names ....
- When I'm losing at football ....
- When people are rude about my family ....
- When people bully my friends ....
- When someone calls me a liar ....
- When someone pushes me ....
- When I get told off and others don't ....
- When things get broken ....
- When someone takes my things ....
- When there is a lot of noise and I'm trying to concentrate. ....
- When I have to do something I don't want to do ....
- When I'm told off in front of my friends ....
- When I get interrupted ....
- When people don't give me a chance ....
- When other people are angry ....
- When people don't listen to me ....
- When people don't understand me ....

Other things that make me angry are:

1. ....

2. ....

3. ....

4. ....

What do I think?

In order to manage our anger we may try to avoid the trigger that sparks us off (as identified in Worksheet 1), but as this is not always possible it is important to have alternative strategies in reacting to the trigger. This involves changing the way we think about the trigger. This gives us more time (a longer fuse) to consider how we will choose to behave.

In Worksheet 2 which follows, a list of incidents are described.

Imagine that these events have happened to you and write down in the first column what you might be thinking that would lead you to be angry.

Then think of some alternative ways in which you might explain the incident that would not lead you to feel angry. It may be helpful to discuss this with a friend or adult. Write this in the second column.

The first two have been completed for you to help you get the idea.

Worksheet 2

What do I think?

Lengthening the fuse!

Trigger *Feelings*	What I think *Angry feelings*	What I think *No angry feelings*
Someone pushes you in the playground.	(i) He wants to pick a fight. (ii) She wants to hurt me.	(i) He lost his balance. (ii) Someone bullied her into it.
Your teacher doesn't listen when you are telling them why you are late.	(i) They don't care about me. (ii) They don't believe me.	(i) She is busy trying to sort out another problem (ii) I have picked a bad time. (iii) I'm not making myself clear.
Your best friend does not talk to you.		
Someone takes your best ruler off your desk.		
You get told off for forgetting your homework.		
Someone shouts at you.		
A friend calls you a liar.		
You are not picked for the school football team.		
A group of children call you names as you walk past them.		

Think about some incidents that have made you angry recently and see if you can change what you think about them.

Keeping calm

When we are teaching young people how to manage their anger more effectively, we know there will be times when we cannot avoid the triggers and we are still learning to change what we think. As young people become more aware of their feelings, thoughts and behaviours, they will become more adept at recognising the signs of anger bubbling. At this stage it will be important for them to identify ways of reducing their levels of arousal in order to reduce the probability of an angry outburst.

To return to the firework analogy, the first Worksheet helped us to reduce the likelihood that the match would be lit, the second Worksheet helped us to lengthen the fuse, allowing more time to consider alternative ways of reacting to triggers, and we will now consider ways to encourage young people to identify their own strong feelings and help them to choose strategies to help reduce their levels of arousal. This could be likened to dampening the fuse and reducing the risk of the explosion.

On Worksheet 3, the pupil will be asked to identify some of their own physiological feelings when they are beginning to feel angry, to help them become more aware of when things are beginning to get out of control for them.

On Worksheet 4, they will then be encouraged to identify what strategies help them to feel better/calm down at those times.

Worksheet 3

How do I feel?

Think about how you feel when you first start to get angry. Tick any of the following statements that apply to you.

I feel hot ....

My hands start to sweat ....

I find it difficult to stay still, I get fidgety ....

My mouth gets dry ....

My hands go into fists ....

My body feels tense ....

My heart races ....

I breathe more quickly ....

I feel panicky ....

Describe three other things that you have noticed about yourself when you are beginning to get angry:

1...

2...

3...

Worksheet 4

Keeping calm

Dampening the fuse!

Here is a list of things that some people do in order to help them to calm down when they recognise the feelings that go along with being angry.

Choose three that you think might work for you and add any of your own that you have thought of or tried.

1. Walking away from the incident.
2. Counting to ten.
3. Talking yourself into feeling calm.
4. Using a catchphrase.
5. Pretending to be somewhere else.
6. Hiding behind an imaginary shield.
7. Using the turtle technique and protecting yourself inside your shell.
8. Take some exercise – running, football, shooting baskets.
9. Have a special place to go.
10. Have a special person to be with.
11. Listen to music
12. Breathe deeply and slowly
13. Relax clenched muscles.

The three that I think I will try, are:

1...

2...

3...

Other things that I do to help me stay calm are..

....

....

Developing a solution

Think about the last time you became really angry. Answer the following questions about it:

What was the trigger?...

What did you think about the incident?..

What did you do to try to keep calm?...

On a scale of 1 to 10, with 1 being the worst it could possibly be, and 10 being the best, *circle the number* that describes how you feel you reacted.

Reacted very badly									*Reacted very well*
1	2	3	4	5	6	7	8	9	10

Assuming you have not circled 1, there must be something about how you behaved that you felt went well – list three of those things below

1...

2...

3...

How could you improve your score by one next time (e.g. from 3 to 4, or 6 to 7) by building on the things that are already going well or by trying new things?

Three things I would do differently next time that would improve my score from .... to ..... are:

1...

2...

3...

Don't forget you do not have to be perfect first time. Just make some changes that you think would be OK for you. If you find this difficult then talk it through with a trusted adult.

Obstacles

Sometimes when we are trying to make changes, things seem to get in the way and make it difficult for us. List below the things that you think will make it difficult for you to make changes:

....

....

....

How could you avoid these obstacles?...

....

....

....

Who could help you with this?

1...

2...

3...

You have now

1. Scored your own behaviour on a scale of 1 to 10.

2. Identified what you are doing well already.

3. Decided what you would like to do to improve your score by one.

4. Thought about what might stop you from making those changes.

5. Identified how you could avoid the obstacles and who could help you with this.

You are now ready to put together your own action plan for improving your anger management.

Action plan

The next time I get really angry the **triggers** are likely to be:

1...

2...

3...

I will try and **avoid** these triggers by

1...

2...

3...

I will know that I am getting angry because I will notice the **signs**:

....

....

....

I will try to **keep calm** by

....

....

....

If I cannot avoid the triggers I will **think differently** about them. My thoughts will be:

....

....

....

I will know that my **behaviour** is better because instead of:

shouting   kicking   throwing things   swearing   damaging things   fighting

other...

(circle the one/s below that fit your behaviour or add your own)

I will   walk away   go to a special place   find someone to talk to

take some exercise   count to ten

other...

I will avoid the **obstacles** to changing my behaviour by:

....

....

....

The **people** I will need to **help** me succeed with this plan are:

1...

2...

3...

Signed.................................Name................................Date ....

96

Appendix 5

Effective anger

Appendices 3 and 4 have helped us to develop the understanding, skills and strategies needed to avoid explosive outbursts of anger that lead to the difficulties associated with problem anger.

The challenge now is how to express anger effectively, in order to provide opportunities to learn and to change. Anger needs to be expressed in a way that respects other people's feelings and points of view, even when they differ from our own. The expression of anger can then be a positive way of resolving conflict and leading to more effective communication between people. In this way relationships can develop and improve as misunderstandings are resolved over time.

Important issues to consider when expressing anger:

Do

- wait until you are calm

- value the other person's point of view, even if you disagree with it

- express your feelings clearly

- offer a solution about how it could be done differently

Don't

- blame the other person

- devalue the other person

- become confrontational

- exaggerate what has happened (i.e. get it out of proportion)

When communicating feelings to others it is useful to separate out the following

- the **behaviour** which has upset us

- the **effect** on our own behaviour

- the **feelings** it has created in us

- the **solution** you would like

For example

For a pupil:

When people .... accuse me of deliberately not doing my homework
(the **behaviour**)

I .... get a detention.
(the **effect**)

It makes me feel .... angry because I feel picked on
(the **feeling**)

I would like to be able to discuss it with you first
(the **solution**)

For a teacher:

When children .... shout out.
(the **behaviour**)

It .... stops me teaching.
(the **effect**)

and makes me feel .... frustrated and short tempered.
(the **feeling**)

I would like you to put your hand up.
(the **solution**)

We can call these '**I Messages**', as we are speaking for ourselves and not blaming others. An example of the difference between an ineffective 'You Message' and an effective 'I Message' would be

For the teacher:

You Message:
'You are always late, why can't you get here on time, I don't know how many times I've told you about this.'

I Message:
'When people are late, it disrupts the lesson and I have to repeat myself. It makes me feel frustrated and disappointed. Could we discuss how to get round this problem later today please?'

For the pupil:

You Message:
'You never play with me, you're horrible and I hate your brother too.'

I Message:
'When children won't play with me, I've got nothing to do and it makes me feel lonely and upset. Is there a game that we could play together?'

I Messages

Write out some effective 'I Messages' for pupils in the following scenarios:

1. Name calling.

    ....

2. Taking toys/equipment without asking...

    ....

3. Spoiling a game...

    ....

4. Being pushed in front of, in a line...

    ....

5. Telling tales...

    ....

6. Copying work...

    ....

7. Being shouted at by a teacher..

    ....

8. Not being noticed when needing help...

    ....

9. Being picked on..

    ....

10. Being told what to do without being told why...

    ....

Don't forget effective messages are important for all of us, teachers, pupils and parents!

Behaviour Modification

GETTING BETTER CHART

.... is getting better

TARGET BEHAVIOUR	MON	TUES	WED	THURS	FRI	SAT	SUN
1							
2							
3							
4							
5							

GO FOR IT!   WELL DONE

Tips for parents of toddlers

As children develop from babyhood to their infant years, they have to deal with strong feelings that have not been experienced before. They are developing by exploring, investigating, watching others, imitating, playing with others, trying out new activities and ideas. There are however, lots of things they cannot do or are not allowed to do at this stage, which can lead to feelings of confusion and frustration. We often expect children to be grown up one minute, 'Be a big girl now . . .' but babies the next, 'You're not old enough to . . .'. Being bossy and 'in charge' is one way in which we cover up feelings of uncertainty and helplessness.

Anger can sometimes be a way of expressing other emotions, fear – for example sadness, frustration. Small children can often feel scared about new situations and people. It is important that we try to understand what the purpose of the anger is.

We all need attention from others, but small children need more than most! It is difficult to switch from getting all the attention a baby gets, to being a toddler/young child, who is expected to play on their own. Children will get the attention that they need in one way or another. If they do not get it when they are 'good', they will continue to behave in a way which gets you by their side. Playing with small children is an important way to show your interest and love. Allowing them to take control of the play, and for you to do it 'their way', is a safe way for children to feel in control of things.

We have learnt our own ways of expressing anger, and how we feel about our children's anger may well be to do with what happened to us as children. It may be difficult for us to let our children express strong emotions effectively if we were not taught to do this ourselves. Children need us to be able to let them express strong feelings whilst still showing we can continue to love and take care of them.

Children learn by example more effectively than from words, so it is important to look at our own ways of expressing strong emotions too. The stresses of having a young family can be high. The demands of babies and young children can lead to feelings of insecurity and depression in adults. We must take time to take care of ourselves as well, by getting support from others where possible. If these normal levels of stress are added to by illness, financial worries, bereavement, relationship difficulties, etc., we can sometimes be left feeling that we are unable to enjoy our children. It is even more difficult to love an angry toddler when we are having difficulties of our own.

Remember

Children must learn that being good is the best way to get your attention.

Expressing angry feelings is normal, children need to feel that they can be upset and angry but still be loved and valued.

Taking care of ourselves is important in helping us to take care of our children.

Do

• Give real choices.

• Turn the task into a game.

• Be honest, even when you think the child won't like it.

• Be clear about what is expected.

• Give time for settling into new or unlocked situations.

• Take it seriously if the child is not ready to manage a difficult situation.

• Think first – don't react too quickly (unless they are in danger).

• Give time for children to discuss things if they are negotiable.

• Give clear warnings well in advance (e.g. bedtime in half an hour).

• Keep your voice calm.

• Avoid battles that are unnecessary.

• Be consistent.

Think about

• Anger is normal – both yours and theirs.

• Sometimes they are feeling muddled and unsure.

• Try to understand what the anger is about – although this is not always easy!

• Anger sometimes covers other feelings e.g. fear, disappointment, frustration, sadness.

• How does their anger make you feel?

• Do you manage to spend some time with your child most days?

• Does your child get more attention from you when they are being naughty or being good?

• Do you and your partner agree on how to manage your child?

• Discussing disagreements between yourself and your partner when your child isn't there.

Don't forget – this is practice for the teenage years!

Tips for parents of primary age children

Most children are adaptable and improve their ability to cope with difficult feelings as they mature. For some, however, it seems particularly difficult to tolerate frustration. This may be a result of a number of factors, personality, learnt patterns of behaviour, emotional stresses, illness.

As children get older it is easier to discuss their difficulties with them. It may be that the reasons for angry outbursts can be identified. Recording angry outbursts and looking at when they happen, and who they happen with, may also help us to find out more about what the anger is about.

At primary level children are continuing to develop their skills through learning both at home and at school. Relationships with siblings and friends become a focus for learning social skills. It is important to encourage children to learn negotiating skills in arguments with friends and family and not to intervene too quickly for them. This will increase their feelings of being in control and managing their own lives successfully.

As children become more able to master new skills effectively, it can sometimes be difficult for them not to expect themselves to get everything 'right' first time. It is important that children learn at this stage that getting things 'wrong' is an important part of learning and does not change their value or worth.

Frustration behaviours can also be seen in children who find if difficult to wait. Children are all individual and some seem to learn to wait effectively without any difficulty, for others, however, it is a skill that needs to be taught.

It is important not to forget that older children, as well as infants, need to feel secure and loved. Although they seem more independent physically and have not yet reached the pressures of adolescence, they still have emotional needs that we must think carefully about. Children do not want to win all the time although they give us that impression! In order to feel secure, it is important that the adults in their lives are able to protect them when they feel unable to do so for themselves. Being firm with children is being kind to them, whereas giving-in will create unhappy, insecure children. It is important that we provide clear rules for children and that we make them explicit. Children also need us to be consistent where possible in order to be sure that we mean what we say. It is helpful too if all the significant adults in the child's life are doing the same things. When schools and families are working together, children have a better chance of changing their behaviour. They also feel secure and confident in the knowledge that all important adults think broadly the same way.

As children mature, they are still using adult role models, so we have a perfect opportunity to show children how to express anger in a non-destructive way, by being calm and assertive. It may be appropriate to ignore the child's angry outburst, but only if you feel that it will not escalate the behaviour and it is safe to do so. It is important to ensure that you are giving plenty of attention when the child is being good. This is not always easy as we are inclined to feel that we can get on with other things when the child is playing/working well. Recognising good behaviour with praise, a cuddle or a treat later in the day is very effective however.

When punishment is needed it is important that it is timely, appropriate and clear what it is for, in order that the child understands what they have done wrong. The severity of the punishment is far less important than the consistency with which it is applied. It is also important to help the child maintain their self-esteem by making it clear that it is the behaviour that is inappropriate and not that the child themselves are 'bad' in some way.

Do
- Where safe, allow children to sort out their own battles, but keep an ear open.
- Wait until you are both calm before you sit down and talk about the angry outbursts.
- Teach your child to ask for help with difficult tasks, before frustration sets in.
- Ignore mild anger if it will not escalate and is safe to do so.
- Allow children to make mistakes and help them to learn from them.
- Help children to learn to wait.
- Stay calm – demonstrate ways of expressing anger that are not destructive.

Think about
- Labelling the behaviour you do not like as inappropriate, rather than the child.
- Providing a consistent approach to dealing with difficult behaviours. Schools and family can support each other by ensuring a consistent approach across all situations. Teachers, special needs assistants, lunch time supervisors, parents – should all be working together to provide consistent messages, rewards and sanctions.
- Sometimes it is more effective to provide small rewards for good behaviour than to punish inappropriate behaviour, but this is only likely to be true when behaviours can be safely ignored. When punishment is needed it will be most effective when
  - it is clearly associated with the behaviour you want to change
  - it is close in time to the event.
  - it is consistently applied – research has sown that punishment does not have to be severe to be effective, but it must be the same each time the behaviour occurs.

Giving some special time to children when you are sharing a task, without criticism or judgement, is very effective in helping children feel valued and emotionally secure.

Tips for parents of teenagers

It is difficult for us to realise that children have developed into young adults and to change our behaviour accordingly. Adolescents are coping with a number of conflicting pressures, success at school/exams, finding an adult identity, maintaining peer relationships, developing sexuality. It is normal for adolescents to push against the boundaries that are set, as they want to take control of themselves and their lives. Adolescents have strong emotional needs however, and the conflicting pressures make it even more important that they feel secure in their usual/known environments, e.g. school/home.

Although we can explain difficult adolescent behaviours by looking at external and internal conflicts, this is not a reason for condoning inappropriate behaviours. Adolescents need the boundaries we set for them in order for them to feel safe. It is important however that they are moving towards self-management and setting their own boundaries as well. Negotiation and compromise are therefore important aspects of relationships between adults and adolescents.

Adolescents are very concerned about 'fairness' so it is important to be consistent in our responses and to discuss our reasons for the limits we are imposing. Young peoples' feelings of needing to 'belong' to a group are very strong at this stage. They will need to belong to a group of friends but also need to feel they belong at home.

Teenagers often give us the impression that their group of friends is more important than their families. This is an outward expression of the conflict of becoming independent whilst still needing emotional support and guidance. It is equally important at this stage that young people know that they are loved and cared for at home.

Teenagers are good at pushing our emotional buttons. If we get upset and over-emotional it is more difficult for us to think effectively and solve problems calmly. Don't be tempted to call names or threaten them with leaving home. Getting angry does not help us solve the problem, or help our relationships, and may lead to punishments that are out of proportion. Young people will learn effective ways of resolving conflicts by example as well as by negotiation.

Living with teenagers can be a difficult and stressful time. We are also having to make the transition from our role as full-time parents to people who have our own lives to lead. This in itself can be a difficult transition time for parents. It is important that we take care of ourselves if we are to be good role models for our children and help them learn effective ways of expressing their angry feelings.

Do

- Listen to their point of view.
- Value their point of view even when you do not agree with it.
- Respond calmly when explaining your point of view.
- Have clear rules, rewards and sanctions.
- Make boundaries explicit and clear.
- Explain the reasons for your rules.
- Negotiate rules together where possible and safe – but be clear when negotiation is not an option.
- Aim for a win/win solution.
- Wait until you are both calm to discuss things.
- Avoid disciplining in anger.
- Avoid making promises/threats that you can not carry out.
- Aim to enforce rules consistently.

Think about

- Although angry outbursts may be directed at you personally, it is helpful to de-personalise them by understanding that you are being asked to provide a boundary. The conflict is probably not between two people but between the young person and authority.
- A major source of conflict between people is poor communication – misunderstanding about intentions, motives, etc., can affect the way we respond. It is important to check that we have understood the young person's point of view and that they have understood ours.
- It is very easy to think they must know what you are thinking or feeling, particularly if you know someone well. It is often necessary to be explicit however, and not make the mistake of thinking that they *must* know what you mean without checking it out.
- It is important to check that there are no extra stresses contributing to the behaviour, e.g. bullying, school work, peer pressure.
- Adolescents are experts at bringing red herrings into an argument! We may find ourselves being taken down an irrelevant track rather than continuing with the request in hand. It may be helpful to employ the broken record technique:

  'Would you tidy your room before you go out please?'
  'I did it yesterday.'
  'Would you tidy your room before you go out please?'
  'You haven't asked . . . to tidy her room!'
  'I am asking you to tidy your room before you go out please!'

  It is very tempting for us to get drawn into a discussion about other issues rather than staying on track. When you are being appropriately assertive, most young people will respond, albeit grudgingly!
- Learning to express strong feelings effectively now, will be good grounding for adult life.

Appendix 10

What children and teachers say about anger

What children say about anger

Children from three different schools were asked:
    What makes you angry?
    What happens when you get angry at home?
    What happens when you get angry at school?
    How do you control your anger?
    The children's responses, which follow, give some firsthand insight into what children think about anger.

What makes you angry?

- When other children kick me.
- When other girls talk about me behind my back.
- When my friend doesn't play with me.
- When no one passes to me in football.
- When I get sums wrong.
- When things take a long time.
- I just do!
- When other people get hurt.
- When I think of hungry/starving children.
- When I don't get enough food.
- When my parents have a 'favourite' in the family.
- When my baby brother gets all the attention.
- When I didn't do anything.
- When the others were doing it as well.
- 'Cause she doesn't like me.
- 'Cause my mum says I'm going to another school.
- 'Cause my mum says you're rubbish.
- When dad throws my toys away.
- When my friend says I can't play.
- When my mum shouts at me to get my coat on.
- Some boys throwing berries at me and I didn't do anything to them.
- The boys who climb up the trees and look in my house.

- When people touch my dinner.
- When someone is beating me at football.
- When someone is nasty to my friends.
- When someone joins in my game without asking.
- When mum shouts.
- When mum doesn't let me watch television.
- When my little sister makes a mess and I have to tidy it up.
- My brother when he pinches my toys/Sister comes in my bed/Brother kicks me/Climbs on me/Spoils my model/Spoils my things.
- When someone hurts them.
- When they can't do something or get something to work.
- When someone stops them doing or having what they want.
- When someone gets angry with them.
- When someone bullies them.

What happens when you get angry at home?

- I get smacked.
- I get the strap/belt.
- I get sent to bed early.
- I lose my pocket money.
- I have my toys taken away from me.
- Mum shouts.
- Mum says I'll get put in a home.
- She don't do nothing.
- She answers a different question.
- Anyway I'm going to live with my dad.
- Tell mum/dad/nan. Punch them/yell at them.
- Smack my dad back.
- Kick the furniture.
- Feel like kicking the door down.
- I shout at the people who make me angry.
- I run around to make me feel better.
- I go away and ignore the person that annoyed me.
- I go to my room and stop talking to mum.
- I call them names and throw mud at them.
- Sometimes I shout.
- I go off and find another friend.
- Tell a dinner lady/teacher. (Don't shout at school or hit out, its dangerous/get told off.)
- Refuse to eat. Go to their room.

What happens when you get angry at school?

- I hit people.
- I'm rude and use bad words.
- I don't talk to anyone.
- I get told off.
- I get detention.
- I get put on a 'step'.
- I get suspended.
- I don't do nothing.
- Grind teeth. Yell or scream. Stamp feet. Cry.

How do you control your anger?

- I could count to 10.
- I breathe deep.
- I run.
- I shout.
- I say a word that's not rude.
- I go and be quiet.
- I get time out.
- I go to the Headteacher.
- Drink of water.
- Think of something that makes me happy.
- Have a lay down and rest.
- Go and play on my own – return when I'm feeling better.
- Give mum a kiss and do as she says.
- Tell your mummy about it.
- Sit down quietly.
- Lie on my bed.
- Go to the shop (forget about it)/Go to the Elephant and Castle (go down the slide there)/Have a cuddle/sweets/treat.
- Tell someone what's made them angry (but they don't always listen).

What teachers say about anger

The same questions were also posed to a group of teachers as a prelude to some in-service training on anger management. Their responses are given below. (How would you answer these questions?)

What makes you angry at work?

- Being asked to do things at very short notice. Being shouted at by staff (not pupils).
- Children – ignored. Staff – not being considered.
- Frustrations regarding time. Working under inconsistent circumstances.

- Pupils mistreating an instrument. Pupils who are rude and mouthy.
- Other people not taking responsibility for their bits. Not completing tasks on time. Criticism.
- Being behind with paperwork – being moaned at for having a messy desk.
- People who insult others or myself. Students who show no respect to colleagues or the environment or the work that is going on.
- People not listening to me. People assuming things before asking. People not doing what I tell them.
- Children who refuse point blank to do what I ask. Rudeness – swearing, challenging requests. Lack of effort – refusal to try.
- Pupils that are deliberately argumentative. Staff asking for work that I see as unnecessary.
- Forced to enforce unenforceable rules. Absences – lack of continuity.
- People letting you down – pupil not bringing in books/work/homework essential to the lesson. Fellow teachers who do not produce work/do items which they should do by required time. Silly behaviour.
- Pupils' deliberate 'winding up' tactics.
- Being put under unnecessary pressure. Not being able to realise my potential due to inflexible management.
- When I have to backtrack and re-work what has been done before.

What makes you angry at home?

- Things like banging my head on a shelf.
- Not being considered.
- Not enough time to achieve goals. Promises not kept by others.
- My partner not helping with the housework.
- My partner sulking.
- Being let down by others, especially friends and family being late when we are going out.
- When there is something that doesn't work, e.g. hot water, heating. When there is no food left.
- People assuming I'll do things before asking me. People wanting my time!
- Pigheadedness. Systematic attempts to wind me up by people who recognise that they are doing so and labour the point. A dirty/untidy house caused by housemates who then wish me to clean it up. A refusal to understand that I am busy/stressed and *can't* socialise with friends during the week. People who waste my time.
- Poor drivers (sometimes). Not a lot!
- Someone not understanding the demands of my job.
- Partner not doing fair share of housekeeping.
- Rarely angry, more frustrated when there seems to be too many things to cope with. Can get angry when family make me late.
- Children not doing something when asked. When equipment goes wrong.
- When my son leaves his dinner plate on the floor and hasn't picked it up 24 hours later.

What happens when you get angry?

- Nothing much usually.
- Stubborn – quiet.
- Analyse and change what can be changed. Talk through and compromise where possible. Accept with shrug that which I cannot affect.
- I want to shout lots.
- At school – with students – calm broken record. With staff, stop, listen. Explode in private. At home – try to explain – shout – plot revenge!
- Try to keep it in. Get all tense and irritable. Usually take it out on the wrong person when eventually it comes out.
- I will become silent and think about it. If I am pushed too far I will shout.
- Tend to get caught up in a situation. Physically or verbally show others around me how I am feeling. Tend to make a situation worse.
- Shouting, single out pupil and tell them their behaviour is unacceptable. Have child removed from room (in extreme circumstances). Home – pointed/nasty comments – personal nasty comments – complete raging behaviour (very occasionally) in which I will scream at someone until I am hoarse and even strike out at them physically. Slamming doors, etc. Throwing things.
- Sometimes I shout, increased body tension.
- Tendency to shout.
- My voice raises.
- At work: give pupil punishment (order or detention) or apply appropriate sanction. Imperative that I don't lose my temper. At home: shout!
- Shout, snap at people.
- I usually go very quiet and walk away. If prompted I become sarcastic.

What do you do to control your anger?

- Let off steam to someone (personally) close to me – not physically close. Rationalise it – think it over and realise it's rather silly to get angry about these things.
- Repress it – in some cases try to justify other person's position to defuse.
- Think.
- Say in my head what I know I *can't* say to the kids. If I'm less stressed I get less angry.
- Physically stop, pause, breath deeply, rationalise why, talk to others, swim, drink red wine!
- Try to talk it through in my own mind – reason, etc. Calm myself down – sometimes has opposite effect. At home – go for a run or go to the gym.
- Talk about it with someone independent of situation.
- Try (and fail) to calm down. Try (and fail) to stand back from a situation.
- Work: step into role, take a step back from the situation, lower my voice, take a deep breath, rational response to what someone is doing to irritate me. Home: leave the room/situation that is bugging me. Exercise – go for a walk or run.

- Exercise to relieve tension. Think about how I can diffuse the situation. Try to put it into context. Walk the dog.
- Slow myself down. Slow my pace.
- Take a deep breath and bite my tongue.
- At work: try to step back from the situation – see whole class. Perhaps ignore source of anger for moment. At home: reason, calm down, start again.
- Consciously take a moment to calm, focus on what *really* matters.
- I usually wink at the kids and make them laugh. I apologise to adults even though I may be right.

What do you do to control your children's anger?

- Put my toddler in her cot and go and talk to her in five minutes. Older children – send them out to calm down. Walk away from them. Talk to them afterwards. Make a little joke with them.
- Drop into immovable object role.
- Talk, rationalise, calm, discuss.
- Send them out to cool off. Settle them elsewhere to work. Send them to another member of staff.
- Listen – don't confront, diffuse – negotiate, delaying tactics, remove audience, suggest practical solutions, build trust.
- Try to encourage to talk. Let them be angry – able to do this during home visit. Give space and time.
- Ask them why they are angry – give them cool off time.
- Try and remove them from one situation. Try to calm them down.
- Lower my voice, ask them to calm down, deep breath, tell me in a sensible way what is making them so cross. If possible separate child from the troublesome situation.
- Try to diffuse the situation by talking softly but being firm.
- Try assertive discipline. Try to know them and find a way to avoid them feeling and demonstrating their anger.
- Talk quietly and calmly to them in the hope it rubs off.
- At work: sometimes giving them space and time to calm down helps, then talk. At home: listen to source of grievance.
- Listen, take time to let them get rid of anger.
- I talk them out of it. Get them to speak slowly and quietly – when calm talk through the situation. Attempt to transcend their self centred view.

References

The following are quoted or referred to in the text

Aristotle, in Goleman, D. (1995).

Beck, A. T. (1976) *Cognitive Therapy and the Emotional Disorders*. New York: International Universities Press.

Beck, A. T. (1988) *Love is Never Enough*. New York: Harper & Row.

Bowlby, J. (1978) *Attachment and Loss*. Harmondsworth: Penguin.

Breakwell, G. M. (1997) *Coping with Aggressive Behaviour*. Leicester: British Psychological Society.

Department for Education (DfE) (1994) *Code of Practice on the Identification and Assessment of Special Educational Needs*. London: HMSO.

Dodge, K. A. (1986) 'A social information processing model of social competence in children', in Perlmutter, M. (ed.), *Cognitive Perspectives on Children's Social and Behavioural Development*, (77–133). Hillsdale, NJ: Lawrence Erlbaum.

Dryden, W. (1996) *Overcoming Anger*. London: Sheldon Press.

Ellis, A. (1994) *Reason and Emotion in Psychotherapy*, 2nd edn. New York: Birch Lane Press.

Erikson, E. H. (1950) *Childhood and Society*. New York: W. W. Norton.

Feindler, E. L. and Ecton, R. B. (1986) *Adolescent Anger Control, Cognitive Behavioural Techniques*. New York: Pergamon Press.

Freud, S. (1967) in Brown, J. *Freud and the Post Freudians*. Harmondsworth: Pelican.

Gardner, H. (1993) *Multiple Intelligences: The Theory in Practice*. New York: Basic Books.

Glasser, W. (1986) *Control Theory in the Classroom*. New York: Harper & Row.

Goleman, D. (1995) *Emotional Intelligence*. London: Bloomsbury Publishing.

Harris et al. (1997) *Physical Interventions: A Policy Framework*. Kidderminster: British Institute of Learning Disabilities (BILD).

Jung, C. (1968) in Fordham, F. (1968) *An Introduction to Jung's Psychology*. Harmondsworth: Penguin.

Kopp, C. B. and Krakow, J. B. (1982) *The Child: Development in a Social Context*. (Bronfenbrenner's Ecological Model, p. 648). USA: Addison-Wesley.

LeDoux, J. (1994) 'Emotion, memory and the brain', *Scientific American* **270**(6), 50–7.

Lyon, C. M. (1994) *Legal Issues*. London: Mental Health Foundation.

Maslow, A. H. (1968) *Towards a Psychology of Being*. New York: Van Nostrand.

National Commission on Education (1996) *Success Against The Odds: Effective Schools in Disadvantaged Areas*. London: Routledge.

Novaco, R. (1978) in Forey and Rathien (eds) *Anger Control: Cognitive Behavioural Intervention*. New York: Plenum Press.

Patterson, G. (1986) 'Performance models for anti-social boys', *American Psychologist* **41**, 432–44.

Potter-Effron, R. (1994) *Angry All the Time: An Emergency Guide to Anger Control*. Oakland, USA: New Harbinger Publications.

Segal, J. (1992) *Melanie Klein*. London: Sage Publication.

Shapiro, L. E. (1994) *The Anger Control Tool Kit*. Pennsylvania: The Center for Applied Psychology.

Bibliography

We acknowledge these authors who have influenced our thinking directly

Aborn, A. (1994) *Why Should I? It's Not My Birthday!* Pennsylvania: Centre for Applied Psychology, Inc.

Apter, T. (1997) *The Confident Child. Emotional Coaching for the Crucial Decade – Ages Five to Fifteen.* New York: W. W. Norton.

Association for Psychological Therapies. Coping with Aggression from Young People in Residential Settings, Conference Report 7th July 1992.

Astor, A. A. (1994) 'Children's moral reasoning about family and peer violence: the role of provocation and retribution', *Child Development* **65**(4), 1054–67.

Dangel, R. F., Deschner, J. P. and Rasp, R. R. (1989) 'Anger control training for adolescent in residential treatment', *Behaviour Modification* **13**(4), 447–73.

Davis, D. L. and Boster L. H. (1992) Cognitive-behavioural-expressive interventions with aggressive and resistant youths', *Child Welfare* **71**(6), 557–73.

Davies, W. and Frude, N. (1993) *Preventing Face to Face Violence.* Leicester: Association for Psychological Therapies.

de Shazer, S. (1985) *Keys to Solutions in Brief Therapy.* New York: W. W. Norton.

Deffenbacher, J. L., Thwaites, G. A., Wallace, T. and Oetting, E. R. (1994) 'Social Skills and Cognitive-Relaxation Approaches to General Anger Reduction', *Journal of Counselling Psychology* **41**(3) 386–96.

Dryden, W. (1968) *Overcoming Anger.* London: Sheldon Press.

Eastman, M. and Craft Rozen, S. (1994) *Taming the Dragon in Your Child.* Chichester: John Wiley.

Gilbert, P. (1997) *Overcoming Depression.* London: Robinson.

Goldstein, A. P. and Glick, B. (1994) 'Aggression replacement training: curriculum and evaluation', *Simulation and Gaming*, March **25**(1), 9–26.

Goldstein, A. P., Carr, E. G. C., Davidson II, W. S. and Wehr, P. (1980). *In Response to Aggression – Methods of Control and Prosocial Alternatives.* New York: Pergamon Press.

Goldstein, A. P., Sprafkin, R. P., Gershaw, N. J. and Klein, P. *Skill-Streaming the Adolescent.* Champaign, Illinois: Research Press.

Helps, V. (1994) *Negotiating – Everybody Wins.* London: BBC Books.

Kellner, M. H. and Tutin, J. A. (1995) 'School-Based Anger Management Programme for Developmentally and Emotionally Disabled High School Students', *Adolescence* **30**(120), 813–25.

Knaus, W. J. (1983) 'Children and low frustration tolerance', in Ellis, A. and Bernard, M. (eds) *Rational Emotive Approaches to the Problems of Childhood*. New York: Plenum.

Kohlberg, L. (1984) *Essays on Moral Development*, Volume 2. *The Psychology of Moral Development*. San Francisco: Harper & Row.

Larson, J. (1994) 'Violence prevention in the schools', *School Psychology Review* **23**(2) 151–64.

Leseho, H. and Howard-Rose, D. (1994) *Anger in the Classroom*. Calgary: Detselig Enterprises.

Levin, D. E. *Teaching Young Children in Violent Times – Building a Peaceable Classroom*. Cambridge, MA: Educators for Social Responsibility.

Lindenfield, G. (1993) *Managing Anger*. London: Harper Collins.

Lochman, J. E., Lampron, L. B., Gemmer T. C. and Harris, S. R. *Anger Coping Intervention with Aggressive Children: A Guide to Implementation in School Settings. Innovations in Clinical Practice: A Source Book (Volume 6)*.

Maag, J. K. and Kotlash, J. (1994) 'Review of stress inoculation training with children and adolescents — Issues and Recommendations', *Behaviour Modification*, **18**(4), 443–69

Mabe, P. A., Treiber, F. A., Riley, W. T., (1992) 'The relationship of anger and child psychopathology', *Child Psychiatry and Human Development* **22**(3), 151–64.

Maiuro, R. D., Vitaliano, P. P. and Cahn, T. S. (1987) 'A brief measure for the assessment of anger and aggression', *Journal of Interpersonal Violence* **2**(2), 166–78

McGinnis, E. and Goldstein, A. P. *Skill-Streaming the Elementary School Child*. Champaign, Illinois: Research Press.

Orpinas, P., Parcel, G. S., McAlister, A. and Frankowski, R., 'Violence prevention in middle schools: a pilot evaluation', *Journal of Adolescent Health* **17**(17), 360–71.

Pollack, G. and Johnson, C. (undated) *My Child Has Temper Tantrums – What Can I Do About It?*

Safran, J. D. (1996) 'Emotion in cognitive–behavioural theory and treatment', in Salkowskis, P. M. (ed.) *Trends in Cognitive and Behavioural Therapy*. (Primary/Secondary/Instrumental Emotions). Chichester: John Wiley.

Shapiro, L. E. *Sometimes I Like to Fight, But I Don't Do It Much Anymore*. Pennsylvania: The Center for Applied Psychology.

Siegel, J. M. 'The Multidimensional Anger Inventory', *Journal of Personality & Social Psychology* **51**, 191–200.

Stern, J. B. and Fodor, I. G. (1989) 'Anger control in children: a review of social skills and cognitive behavioural approaches to dealing with aggressive children', *Child & Family Behaviour Therapy* **11**, 3–4, 1–20.

Resources

Allen, B. (1994) *If It Makes My Life Easier . . . To Write a Policy on Behaviour*. Bristol: Lame Duck Publishing. *How to . . . write a policy.*

Anger Solution Game (1995) Center for Applied Psychology Inc, King of Prussia, Pennsylvania, 19406. *Board Game for use in running anger management groups.*

Apsland, G. (1994) *Feelings, Stories for Assembly and P.S.E.* Crediton: Southgate Publishers Limited. *A collection of some 15 stories, dealing with such issues as fairness, friendship, responsibility, aimed at Primary level.*

Cowie, H. and Sharp, S. (eds) (1996) *Peer Counselling in Schools – a time to listen*. London: David Fulton Publishers. *For students to help each other improve interpersonal relationships.*

Herbert M. (1994) *Setting Limits*. Devon: Impact Desktop Publications. *Advice for teachers.*

Hitchen, P. and Hunt, J. (1991) *Dilemmas*. Bristol: Lucky Duck Publishing. *Real-life problem solving exercises for personal, social and moral education.*

Lake, M. (1996) *Zeto and the Gorgon Warriors. Using the notion of the classroom group as a 'Community of Enquiry'*. Birmingham: The Questions Publishing Company. *This 'novel' or story is designed to provoke reflection – used with top primary or lower secondary pupils.*

Lee, J. (1993) *Facing the Fire. Experiencing and Expressing Anger Appropriately*. New York: Bantam Books. *Helping adults to understand and manage anger.*

Lissaman, S. and Riley, E. (undated). *Making a difference – Developing social behaviour in young children*. Stockton-on-Tees: Education Department. *Four sections provide a synopsis of research findings to develop practical activities in the classroom*

Long, R. (1995) *Making Sense of Teenagers*. Devon County Council. *A radical publication – advice for teachers/parents.*

Lucky Duck Publishing (1996) *Working With Challenging Behaviour*. Bristol. *Training and policy development materials.*

Maglish, E. and Maglish, F. (1980) *How To Talk So Kids Will Listen and Listen So Kids Will Talk*. New York: Rawson-Wade.

Maines, B. and Robinson, G. (1994) *If It Makes My Life Easier ... To Write a Policy on Bullying*. Bristol: Lame Duck Publishing. *How to . . . write a policy.*

McKay, M., Fanning, P., Paleg, K. and Landis, D. (1996) *When Anger Hurts Your Kids. A Parent's Guide.* Oakland, Calif.: New Harbinger. *Outlining the effects of parental anger, before offering a detailed plan of action for parents to change the way they think, what they do and how they speak to their children.*

Mitchell, G. (1997) *Practical Strategies for Individual Behaviour Difficulties.* London: David Fulton Publishers. *Practical advice for teachers . . . early intervention programmes*

Moss, G., Came, F., Webster, A. (1997) *Behaviour Education. Teaching positive behaviour in the Primary School.* Bristol: Avec Designs Ltd. *Useful resource for whole school policy and curriculum issues.*

Searle, Y. and Streng, I. (1996) *The Anti-Bullying Game.* London: Jessica Kingsley Publishers. *These games are described as 'therapeutic board games'; It is essential that they are always used in the presence and guidance of a teacher or experienced adult, or better still by psychologists.*

Shapiro, L. E. (1995) *The Anger Control Survival Kit.* The Center for Applied Psychology, Inc., King of Prussia, Pennsylvania 19406. *Practical activities for training and a resource for teachers, psychologists and others (for 5 to 16 years).*

Sunderland, M. and Engleheart, P. (1993) *Draw On Your Emotions – Creative Ways to Explore, Express and Understand Important Feelings.* Bicester, Oxon: Winslow Press. *Contains 'easy-to-do' picture exercises designed to facilitate children talking about their feelings: can be adapted for a wide age range.*

The Antidote (1997) *Realising the Potential: Emotional Education For All.* Antidote, The Hub, 3–4 Albion Place, Galena Road, London W6 0QT. *Curriculum for developing emotional literacy with children.*

Books for use with children (3 to 10 years)

Aborn, A. (1994) *Why Should I? It's Not my birthday!* and *Everything I do you blame on me* (two books in one) – *A choose-your-own Solution Book.* Pennsylvania: The Center for Applied Psychology, Inc.

Sandak, M. (1963) *Where the Wild Things Are.* New York: Harper & Row.

Shapiro, L. E. (1994) *The Very Angry Day that Amy Didn't Have.* Pennsylvania: Center for Applied Psychology, Inc.

Shapiro, L. E. (1995) *Sometimes I Like to Fight, But I Don't Do It Much Anymore.* Pennsylvania: Center for Applied Psychology, Inc.

Watson, J. and Switzer, R. (1986) *Sometimes I get angry.* Kansas: Merringer Press.

Index